Believer's
BIBLE
DOCTRINE
Handbook

Andrew W. Wilson

Believer's Bible Doctrine Handbook: Eighty Christian Truths

Copyright © 2018 Andrew W. Wilson

Believers Publications, P. O. Box 485, North Lakes, Queensland, 4509, Australia

All rights reserved. No part of this publication may be reproduced or transmitted in any form or by any means, electronic or mechanical, including photocopy, recording or otherwise, except for brief quotations in printed reviews, without the written permission of the publisher.

Scripture quotations, unless otherwise noted, are taken from the New King James Version, copyright © 1979, 1980, 1982 by Thomas Nelson, Inc. Used by permission. All rights reserved.

Scripture quotations marked (KJV) are taken from The Holy Bible, Authorized King James Version

Scripture quotations marked (ESV) are taken from The Holy Bible, English Standard Version® (ESV®), copyright © 2001 by Crossway Bibles, a publishing ministry of Good News Publishers. Used by permission. All rights reserved.

Scripture quotations marked (NIV) are taken from the Holy Bible, New International Version®, NIV®, copyright © 1973, 1978, 1984, 2011 by Biblica, Inc.™ Used by permission of Zondervan. All rights reserved worldwide. www.zondervan.com The "NIV" and "New International Version" are registered in the United States Patent and Trademark Office by Biblica, Inc.™

ISBN: 978-0-9943977-3-7

CONTENTS

Acknowledgments and Abbreviations   1

SECTION ONE: SCRIPTURE

1	Ten Reasons to Believe the Bible is the Word of God	4
2	The Inspiration of Scripture	6
3	The Inerrancy of Scripture	8
4	The Authority of Scripture	10
5	The Sufficiency and Necessity of Scripture	12
6	The Illumination of Scripture	14
7	The Canon of Scripture	16

SECTION TWO: GOD

8	Ten Reasons for Believing in God	20
9	Who is God?	22
10	God's Attributes: Eternal	24
11	God's Attributes: All-Powerful	26
12	God's Attributes: Spiritual	28
13	God's Attributes: Personal	30
14	God's Attributes: All-Knowing	32
15	God's Attributes: Holy	34
16	God's Attributes: Loving	36
17	God's Attributes: Perfect	38
18	The Trinity	40
19	God's Servants : Angels	42
20	God's Enemies: Satan and Demons	44

SECTION THREE: CHRIST

21	The Deity of Christ	48
22	The Humanity of Christ	50
23	The Virgin Birth	52
24	The Sinlessness of Christ	54
25	The Mystery of Christ's Person	56
26	Christ's Death	58
27	The Atonement	60
28	Reasons to Believe in the Resurrection	62
29	The Doctrine of the Resurrection	64

SECTION FOUR: THE HOLY SPIRIT

30	The Person of the Holy Spirit	68
31	The Work of the Holy Spirit	70
32	The Holy Spirit and the Believer	72
33	The Baptism in the Holy Spirit	74
34	The Filling of the Spirit	76
35	The Gifts of the Spirit	78

SECTION FIVE: MAN

36	The Doctrine of Man	82
37	Man's Origin	84
38	Man's Purpose	86
39	Human Destiny	88
40	Male and Female	90
41	Human Nature	92

SECTION SIX: SIN

42	The Doctrine of Sin	96
43	Sin's Origin	98
44	Sin's Consequences	100

SECTION SEVEN: SALVATION

45	The Doctrine of Salvation	104
46	Justification	106
47	New Birth	108
48	Faith	110
49	Faith and Works	112
50	Human Responsibility	114
51	Election	116
52	Eternal Security	118
53	Assurance of Salvation	120
54	Baptism	122

SECTION EIGHT: SANCTIFICATION

55	Sanctification	126
56	Consecration	128
57	The Christian and the Law	130

58	Walking in the Spirit	132
59	The Christian and Grace	134
60	Union with Christ	136

SECTION NINE: THE CHURCH

61	The Church	140
62	The Mission of the Church	142
63	Church Government	144
64	Church Unity	146
65	Church Leadership	148
66	Church Characteristics	150
67	The Lord's Supper	152
68	Church Participation	154

SECTION TEN: FUTURE EVENTS

69	What Most Christians Agree On	158
70	Paradise Restored	160
71	The Millennium	162
72	Three Views on Future Events	164
73	Daniel 9: The Key to Future Events	166
74	Israel's Future	168
75	The Tribulation	170
76	The Antichrist	172
77	Armageddon	174
78	The Rapture	176
79	What Christ said about the Future	178
80	The Church and the Tribulation	180

| | Endnotes | 182 |

ACKNOWLEDGMENTS

I want to thank my family for their help with this book; particularly my father, my wife Gill, and my son John. They have improved the ideas and final form of the book. My son Tim also helped with layout. I want to thank all the students whom I have taught Systematic Theology at GLO College of Ministries, Smithton, Tasmania. This book takes the form of notes that were originally written for their benefit and refined in the classroom. In addition, I want to thank numerous churches where I have been privileged to preach on doctrinal topics over the last few years, particularly my home church: Wavell Heights Christian Assembly, Brisbane. Lastly, I want to thank God for the privilege of studying His Word and being given help to appreciate something of the 'unsearchable riches of Christ' (Eph. 3:8).

ABBREVIATIONS

cf.	compare with
Darby	J. N. Darby's New Translation
ESV	English Standard Version
Gk.	Greek
Heb.	Hebrew
KJV	King James Version
lit.	literally
LXX	Septuagint (Greek translation of the Hebrew Scriptures)
NIV	New International Version
NKJV	New King James Version
NT	New Testament
OT	Old Testament
RV	Revised Version

Contend earnestly for the faith which was once for all delivered to the saints

Jude 3

SECTION ONE:

The Doctrine of Scripture

1 TEN REASONS TO BELIEVE THE BIBLE IS THE WORD OF GOD

1.   **The Bible Claims to be the Word of God.** The Bible does not present us with a few, scattered places which hesitatingly point to the possibility that the Bible is of divine origin, but instead gives us a torrent of texts testifying to God's inspiration (e.g. 'Thus says the Lord' occurs over 400 times; it is called the 'oracles of God', Rom. 3:2, 'the Law of the Lord', Ps. 19:7, 'Your (God's) Word', John 17:17). The fact that the Bible claims to be the Word of God does not prove that it is, but is important because if the Bible never claimed to be the Word of God, or its claims were weak or vague, then we would have little confidence in it. But on the contrary, the Bible consistently testifies to its own inspiration (2 Tim. 3:16, 2 Pet. 1:20-21, Hos. 1:1, Mic. 1:1, Acts 1:16, 4:25, 1 Tim. 5:18, Heb. 3:7, 2 Pet. 3:15-16).

2.   **The Bible's Permanence.** Despite being banned, burned, criticised and mocked more than any other book, the Bible has survived for over 3000 years. The reason for the Bible's permanence is because it is *'the word of God which lives and abides forever'* (1 Pet. 1:23). 'A thousand times over, the death knell of the Bible has been sounded, the funeral procession formed, the inscriptions cut on the tombstone, and the committal read. But somehow the corpse never stays put' (Ramm)[1].

3.   **The Popularity of Scripture.** The Bible remains the world's best-selling book. Despite being written thousands of years ago, the Bible has universal appeal. It is read and loved by millions of people of all countries, ages, classes and cultures. The Bible is not a dry, old, dusty relic of another age – a dead book – it is the living Word of God.

4.   **The Unity of the Bible.** The sixty-six books of the Bible were written by more than 30 different human authors, living on different continents, from different classes of society, over a period of 1,500 years. Nevertheless, the books these authors left to us in the Bible are a harmonious unity, pointing to one divine mind behind the Bible.

5.   **The Fulfilled Prophecies of the Bible.** The Bible is full of prophecies about the future. For example, there are over 300 different

prophecies relating to the Messiah fulfilled in the life of Jesus Christ. Professor Peter Stoner studied eight of these prophecies and calculated the probability of someone fulfilling just eight of the prophecies as one in a hundred million billion[2]. Fulfilled prophecy points to a divine author behind the Bible (see Isa. 46:9-10).

6. **The Historical Accuracy of Scripture.** Critics have argued that the Bible is full of fables, but many of the Bible's kings, cities and events have been confirmed by historians. W. F. Albright, the greatest authority on Biblical archaeology of his day, wrote 'There can be no doubt that archaeology has confirmed the substantial historicity of Old Testament tradition'[3].

7. **The Scientific Accuracy of the Bible.** Sceptics claim that the Bible is full of pre-scientific myths and absurdities. However, while ancient cultures believed the earth rested on the back of an elephant (Hindus), a catfish (Japanese), or on one of the gods (Greeks), the Bible teaches that the earth hangs upon nothing (Job 26:7). The Bible also tells us that the stars cannot be counted (Gen. 22:17, Jer. 33:22), despite less than 5000 stars being visible to the naked eye. The reason the Bible managed to get these scientific facts correct is because its author is God.

8. **The Character of the Human Authors.** 2 Peter 1:21 assures us that the human writers of Scriptures were 'holy men of God'. The holiness of the writers (they were not charlatans), and their plural number (rather than one sole writer, like the Koran, or the book of Mormon) give us more reasons we can trust the Scriptures they wrote.

9. **Christ's Testimony to Inspiration.** If Christ rose from the dead, and is the Son of God who cannot lie, the fact that He repeatedly attested to Scripture as God's Word (Matt. 4:4, 5:17-18, 22:43, Mark 7:13, John 10:35) means that the most important reason for believing the Bible is God's Word is because the Son of God said it was.

10. **The Living Power of the Bible.** God speaks to us through the Bible in living power. *'The word of God is living and powerful, sharper than any two-edged sword'* (Heb. 4:12). The final reason for believing that the Bible is God's Word is an experience – we realise that God is speaking to us from the Bible. The Bible is thus self-authenticating.

2 THE INSPIRATION OF SCRIPTURE

The Inspiration of Scripture means that the Bible is God's Word. Although its various books were written by human authors, their writing was infallibly supervised by the Holy Spirit in such a way that all the words in the original autographs are truly the words of God.

1. Inspiration means 'God-breathed' (2 Tim. 3:16). Scripture did not originate with human authors, but with the Holy Spirit (2 Pet. 1:21). The Bible is God's Word (Matt. 4:4, 22:43, Mark 7:13, John 10:35).
2. Verbal inspiration – the very words are inspired (Matt. 5:18, Exodus 34:27, 2 Sam. 23:2, Prov. 30:5, Jer. 1:9, 36:2, 28).
3. Plenary (*full, entire*) Inspiration – the entire Bible is God's Word (Luke 24:44, 2 Tim. 3:16, Psalm 119:160).
4. Dual Authorship – the Bible is both God's Word and man's words. The Bible is not part-human and part-Divine, but fully God's Word and fully man's words.
5. Only the text of the original autographs is inspired, not later copies or translations, which are inspired to the degree that they faithfully represent the original wording of the Bible.

WRONG IDEAS ABOUT INSPIRATION: WHAT IT DOES NOT MEAN:

a. **A 'Creative Spark'**: inspiration is not a 'creative influence', like what might prompt an artist, composer or poet. The word 'inspiration' instead means 'God-breathed' (Gk. *theopneustos*, 2 Tim. 3:16).
b. **Natural Inspiration**: the Bible is not just a work of genius written by naturally-gifted people.
c. **Inspirational**: 'inspiration' is sometimes (mis)understood to mean the Bible is 'uplifting' or 'encouraging' in its effect on readers, but while it is true that this happens, this is not what inspiration means.
d. **The Bible *contains* the Word of God**: some teach that the Bible contains the Word of God (along with errors). However, 'all Scripture is inspired by God', not just parts of it.
e. **General Inspiration**: some teach that the Bible's general concepts (God, 'the golden rule') are inspired, but not its words. However, it is impossible to clearly convey concepts without words.

f. **Partial Inspiration**: some argue the Bible is inspired in spiritual matters, but not in history or science; it is a mixture of truth and error. But the Bible's spiritual message depends upon its historical record. To deny one is to undermine the other.
g. **Relative Inspiration**: some believe that certain parts of the Bible are more inspired than others (e.g. the words of Jesus). But while the words of Christ are the very heart of the Christian faith, all Scripture is God's Word. We must not set up a 'canon within the canon'.
h. **Neo-Orthodox Inspiration**: some have taught that certain parts of the Bible *become* God's Word when God speaks through them to us. However, Christ taught that the Bible is 'the Word of God' (Mark 7:8-13, John 10:35). The fact that God speaks in living power through the Bible should lead us to place our full trust in it.
i. **Mechanical Inspiration**: it was all dictated word for word by God. While some parts of the Bible were dictated (e.g. Rev. 2:1), yet other parts are from eyewitness records (Luke 1:1-4) or recollection (John 14:26). If all was dictated, the styles of the books would be identical.
j. **Only Certain Translations are Inspired**: e.g. the KJV, Latin Vulgate. The apostles did not use these later translations, nor are these versions perfect[4] (there were 75,000 changes between the 1611 and 1769 KJV); only the original texts of the Bible are inspired.

Summary: Christ attests plenary, verbal inspiration in Matt. 4:4: 'every (plenary) word (verbal) that proceeds from God's mouth (inspiration)'. 'The inspiration of Scripture is plainly affirmed therein, but its process will ever remain a mystery ... The inspiration of Scripture is far different from that of a great poet or painter. Nor is it mere mechanical dictation. That would destroy 'the human element' which we discern throughout it. Like the Living Word, the Lord Jesus (who indeed is the very heart of the Scripture), the Bible is at once divine and human' (E. W. Rogers[5]).

'When we read the Bible, God is speaking'. It is 'profitable for doctrine, reproof, correction, instruction' (2 Tim. 3:17). 'The Holy Spirit is not only the Primary Author of Scripture, but also, in Abraham Kuyper's phrase, the Perpetual Author, continually speaking through the Word to the believing reader and unfolding fresh meaning from it' (F. F. Bruce[6]).

3 THE INERRANCY OF SCRIPTURE

The Inerrancy of Scripture means that the Bible is true and without error in all that it teaches. **Biblical Basis:** God can neither lie (Num. 23:19, Tit. 1:2) nor make errors (Ps. 147:5, Isa. 40:28), so it follows that His inspired Word (2 Tim. 3:16) is without error. Christ affirmed the inerrancy of Scripture: 'Your word is truth' (John 17:17), 'Scripture cannot be broken' (John 10:35). Psalm 12:6 says 'the words of the LORD are pure words, like silver ... purified seven times' (see also Prov. 30:5, and Ps. 119:140). See also 2 Sam. 22:31, Psalm 19:7, 9b, 119:142, 160 ('entirely true'). Dan. 10:21 calls them the 'Scriptures of truth'.

WRONG IDEAS ABOUT INERRANCY

Limited Inerrancy: the Bible is true in what it says about spiritual matters, but it may contain mistakes in scientific or historical matters. However, if the Bible is not true in earthly matters (which we can check), how can we know it is true in spiritual matters (cf. John 3:12)?

Accommodation: Christ accommodated himself to the prevailing (wrong) ideas of His day. However, Christ was 'the truth' (John 14:6), God's 'faithful witness' (Rev. 1:5). Christ constantly affirmed (instead of ignored) Bible stories and based spiritual truths upon them. E.g. Creation, Adam and Eve (Mark 10:6-9, 13:19), Noah's flood, Sodom (Luke 17:26-27, 29), Jonah (Matt. 12:39-41), Daniel (Matt. 24:15).

CLARIFICATIONS AND QUALIFICATIONS

The Bible contains the following phenomena:

Reporting of Falsehoods: sometimes the Bible reports untruths: 'There is no God' (Ps. 14:1) or Satan's lie in the Garden of Eden (Gen. 3:4).

Everyday Language: 'the language of appearance', e.g. 'the sun rises' (Psalm 104:22). This is not false; it is the way it truly appears.

Figurative Language: not 'literally true', e.g. Pharisees 'devour widows' houses' (Matt. 23:14), false-prophets are 'ravenous wolves' (Matthew 7:15). 'The pillars of the earth' (1 Sam. 2:8, Job 9:6) are figurative expressions; cf. Job 26:7, 'He hangs the earth on nothing'.

Approximations: e.g. feeding of the 5000. Approximations are not false, and are often necessary, e.g., the circumference of the bronze sea in Solomon's Temple was 30 cubits (13.5m), diameter 10 cubits, 4.5m (2 Chron. 4:2), but a circle with a diameter of 4.5m cubits multiplied by *pi* (3.14159) would have a circumference of 14.14m (not 13.5).

Translation Issues: Some biblical words have a double meaning. E.g. in Acts 9:7, the men who accompanied Saul were 'speechless, *hearing a voice but seeing no one*', while in Acts 22:9, Paul says that those with him 'saw the light ... but *they did not hear the voice* of Him who spoke to me'. It is possible to hear a sound, but not what was said. In Acts 22:9, the Greek text shows that the men did not apprehend what was said.

Copying Mistakes: Our Bibles sometimes contain scribal copying errors, e.g. Solomon's horses (1 Kings 4:26, 2 Chron. 9:25), Ahaziah's age (2 Kings 8:26, 2 Chron. 21:20). Ancient manuscripts and context help us to restore the original, correct, reading.

Selective Use of Material: Bible writers selectively include material (see John 20:30), and shorten it, e.g. Matthew does not tell us about the roof being broken up for the paralyzed man (Matt. 9:2, cf. Mark 2:4).

Author's Intention: We need to understand the reason why a biblical writer tells us something, before trying to answer our own questions (e.g. Judas' death 'contradiction', Matt. 27:5, cf. Acts 1:18).

DIFFICULTIES IN SCRIPTURE

If we come up against a Bible difficulty, we should pray for God's Spirit to help us understand His Word, and patiently wait on Him. Other passages will help explain the one we are reading. Sometimes, we need to grow spiritually before we can understand God's Word. Augustine wrote, 'I have learnt, I confess, to pay such deference to the books of Scripture, and to them alone, that I most firmly believe that none of their writers has ever fallen into any error in writing. And if I meet with anything in them which seems to me to be contrary to truth, I doubt not that either the manuscript is in fault, or that the translator has missed the sense, or that I myself have not rightly apprehended it'[7].

4 THE AUTHORITY OF SCRIPTURE

The Authority of Scripture means that because the Bible is God's written Word, Christians should allow it to govern their lives by believing and obeying it. **Biblical Basis**: Christ turned to Scripture to settle any question (cf. Mt. 4:4); He criticized the Pharisees for not following it (e.g. Mt 12:3, 5; 19:4, 21:16, 22:31, Mark 2:25, 12:26). Christ gave Scripture greater authority than tradition (Mk. 7:1-13), reason (Matt. 22:31) or experience, (Luke 16:29-31). In the epistles, the apostles quote Scripture to prove a point (e.g. 'for/as it is written' or 'for the Scripture says' or 'what says the Scripture?'). Various NT books appeal to the authority of Scripture to establish their arguments, for example, Rom. 3 quotes seven OT verses to prove the sinfulness of man, and Gal. 3 uses seven quotes to establish that justification is by faith not works.

ALTERNATIVES TO BIBLICAL AUTHORITY

Tradition: what has been handed down from one generation to another. Thus, the Roman Catholic church and Eastern Orthodox churches claim that church tradition must either be placed alongside Scripture on an equal footing or as a supplementary authority.

Reason: the human ability to think and understand. Liberal theologians reject supernatural events in Scripture (miracles, predictive prophecy) because they believe that modern scientific progress means we cannot any longer accept myths or 'primitive superstitions'. However, human reasoning is limited; sin's corruption extends to our thinking, and there are many things we do not know. 'The mind of the creature cannot measure the Creator' (Milne[8]). Proverbs 3:5 warns us, 'Trust in the Lord with all your heart, and lean not on your own understanding'.

Experience: the human ability to observe, feel and remember events. Charismatic Christianity often places emotions, intuitions, dreams, personal revelations and ecstatic experiences alongside Scripture as equally authoritative. However, not all experiences are from God, nor is the Holy Spirit ever 'contrarious to Himself' (John Knox); the Author of Scripture will never 'go beyond' (1 Cor. 4:6 ESV) what is written in it.

Scripture must be given the place of ultimate authority as God's inspired Word. Its authority trumps human tradition, human reasoning, or human experiences. Isaiah 8:20 says, 'To the law and to the testimony! If they do not speak according to this word, it is because there is no light in them'. 'Men must either deny that the Bible is the Word of God, or admit its sufficiency and supremacy in all ages' (C. H. Mackintosh[9]). Augustine: 'If you believe what you like in the gospel, and reject what you don't like, it is not the gospel you believe, but yourself'.

NOT OUR ONLY AUTHORITY, BUT OUR ULTIMATE AUTHORITY

It is a mistake to say that Scripture is our only authority. We gladly accept that tradition, reason and experience have some authority and validity, and we are all influenced to some degree by them. However, if the Bible is God's inspired Word, it must also be our ultimate authority, by which we test any tradition, argument or experience.

Tradition: For example, the word Trinity is not found in the Bible, nor is it a recent invention, but we are happy to agree that the word nicely sums up what the Bible teaches us about God.

Reason: Paul reasoned in the synagogues as he preached the gospel (Acts 17:17, 18:4, etc.), God says, 'Come now, and let us reason together' (Isa. 1:18), and we need to meditate on Scripture, that is, to think about it.

Experience: We should have an experience of God in our lives, converting and changing us. The Bible itself says, 'Oh, taste and see that the Lord is good, blessed is the man who trusts in Him' (Psalm 34:8).

OTHER SOURCES OF AUTHORITY

Biblical Scholarship: some bow down before commentaries ('paper popes'), celebrity preachers, creeds, catechisms, and confessions. These sources of authority are only dependable insofar as they follow Scripture.

Delegated Authority: Human government, Church government, parents. These God-given positions have legitimate but limited authority, restricted by Scripture; 'we ought to obey God rather than men' (Acts 5:29).

5 THE SUFFICIENCY AND NECESSITY OF SCRIPTURE

The Sufficiency of Scripture means that the Bible provides all that we need for faith and conduct as Christians. **Biblical Basis**: Christ told the disciples that 'when He, the Spirit of truth, has come, He will guide you into *all truth*' (John 16:13, cf. 14:26). Jude 1:3 speaks about 'the faith *once for all* delivered to the saints'. 2 Tim. 3:15-17 says that Scripture is inspired by God with the result 'that the man of God may be *complete, thoroughly* equipped for *every* good work'. 2 Peter 1:3-4 tell us that God's 'divine power has given to us *all things* that pertain to life and godliness'. Psalm 19:7 says, 'The law of the LORD is perfect (i.e. complete), converting the soul, the testimony of the LORD is sure, making wise the simple'. James 1:25 calls God's Word 'the perfect law of liberty'. Various verses warn us against adding to, or taking away from, Scripture: Deut. 4:2, 5:22, 12:32, Proverbs 30:5-6, Rev. 22:18-19.

DENIALS OF THE SUFFICIENCY OF SCRIPTURE

Additions to Scripture: The doctrine of the sufficiency of Scripture means that we should not add other books or doctrines to what Scripture teaches:

- the Roman Catholic church has added extra doctrines to what Scripture teaches, like indulgences, purgatory, papal infallibility and praying to saints.
- The Church of Jesus Christ of Latter-Day Saints have added other books to Scripture (for example, the *Book of Mormon*).
- The 'Doctrine of Development' (J. H. Newman, 1845) argued that the early church grew out of its primitive, infant stage and that later doctrinal developments were natural and to be expected (thus justifying various Catholic doctrines not found in the Bible). Anglican writers similarly argue for a doctrine of development in relation to the church government, justifying the second century rule by monarchical bishops as a natural development.
- Some charismatic Christians have argued that the Scriptures are not sufficient because we also need signs and wonders, or extra revelations.

MISUNDERSTANDINGS OF THE SUFFICIENCY OF SCRIPTURE
Scripture is Sufficient, but not Exhaustive:
1. The Scriptures are not sufficient for life in general (e.g. they do not teach us how to cook a meal, or how to fix our car).
2. Scripture is not exhaustive in what it teaches us about God (Deut. 29:29 says that 'the secret things belong to the Lord').
3. Scripture does not give exhaustive teaching about our Christian lives (e.g. who to marry, what career or job to take, etc.).
4. The NT is not exhaustive about church life: it does not tell us what hymn book to use, what time to meet, etc.

Scripture is Not the Only Way that God Speaks Today
- God speaks to unbelievers and believers through Creation (Psalm 19), providence (God's care), answered prayer, conscience, our gospel witness, the Holy Spirit's encouragement through fellowship with other believers, etc.
- God guides His people (Psalm 48:14, 73:24, Isa. 58:11, Acts 16:6, Rom. 1:10, Col 1:9) through Scripture, wisdom, advice from other Christians and through circumstances.
- The sufficiency of Scripture does not deny that God can intervene in His world, or that He also speaks in other ways. However, it insists that Scripture is supreme. No other 'message from God' is inspired, inerrant or authoritative; only Scripture is a certain Word from God, the standard by which we evaluate all else. If a dream about evangelism is a prompt from God, what is a dream about robbing a bank a few nights later? We must test everything by God's Word.

THE NECESSITY OF SCRIPTURE
The necessity of Scripture means that we cannot do without the Bible, for what it teaches is essential for the faith and practice of believers
Biblical Basis: Christ quoted Deut. 8:3 in Matt. 4:4: 'man shall not live by bread alone but by every word that proceeds from the mouth of God'.

We deny the necessity of Scripture by arguing that the teachings of the Bible are not necessary or normative for faith or practice today.

6 THE ILLUMINATION OF SCRIPTURE

The doctrine of the clarity of Scripture was formulated at the time of the Reformation as a reaction to the refusal of the Roman Catholic church to allow ordinary people to read the Bible for themselves, and because its official teachings contradicted the plain teaching of Scripture on important matters (e.g. selling forgiveness of sins for money, and salvation by works). The clarity of Scripture means we do not need a class of special interpreters (like priests or professors), to understand the Bible. It is not only highly educated people who can understand the Bible, but all people, young and old (Deut. 4:9, 6:6-7, 11:18-19, 2 Tim. 3:15). The claim that the Bible is impossible to understand is not true.

However, there are also difficult things in the Bible. Even Peter says that Paul's writings have 'some things hard to understand' (2 Pet. 3:16). Other parts of the Bible are not so easy to understand either; there are few who think Revelation is straightforward reading. Bible-believing Christians also disagree on many points despite having the same Bible.

The Illumination of Scripture means that we can understand God's Word through the teaching of the Holy Spirit, our meditation upon it, and fellowship with other saints. **Biblical Basis:** The psalmist prayed, 'Open my eyes that I may see wondrous things from Your law' (Ps. 119:18; see also later verses in the same psalm: vs33-34, 102). In the NT, Christ taught that understanding of spiritual truth is dependent on God's revelation (Matt. 11:25-27). He quoted the words of the OT, 'they shall all be taught by God' (John 6:45). In 1 Cor. 2:10 Paul teaches that it is only by the Holy Spirit's work that we can understand the truths of God: 'God has revealed them (spiritual truths) to us through His Spirit'. In Eph. 1:17, Paul prays that God might 'give to you the spirit of wisdom and revelation in the knowledge of Him'. See also 1 John 2:20.

QUALIFICATIONS

However, the doctrine of the Illumination of Scripture needs to be carefully qualified.

1. There is a **spiritual** element to understanding Scripture. The Holy Spirit is the Church's teacher (John 14:26, 16:13). Without spiritual illumination, it is impossible to receive scriptural truth. Unspiritual people cannot receive God's Word (1 Cor. 2:6-7, 14-16).
2. There is an **intellectual** element to understanding Scripture. We must meditate in God's Word, reading it and studying it carefully, prayerfully and regularly. Occasional, cursory reading is not enough (Josh. 1:8, Psalm 1:2).
3. There is a **moral** element to understanding Scripture. We must be willing to obey Scripture to properly understand it (John 7:17, Psalm 111:10). If we do not act on the light that God has given us, why should God give us more light?
4. There is a **communal** element to understanding Scripture. God has placed us in the Church so that 'we all come to the unity of the faith ... [by] ... speaking the truth in love' (Eph. 4:13-15, cf. Prov. 27:17). By contrast, 'A man who isolates himself seeks his own desire; he rages against all wise judgment' (Prov. 18:1). The illumination of Scripture does not mean that we have no need of teachers in the Church. Instead, we need each other to grow in understanding.
5. Not everything in the Bible is easy to understand (2 Peter 3:15-16). There is milk for spiritual babes, as well as meat for the spiritually mature (1 Cor. 3:2, Heb. 5:12-14).
6. Because we do not know everything (1 Cor. 8:2), we need to be humble in our interaction with other Christians about what Scripture means; (a) we might be wrong, (b) we might learn from others, or (c) we might be able to help them.

Why do People Differ in their Understanding of Scripture?

Differing interpretations of Scripture almost always arise from the prejudices, partial insights, presuppositions and problems that we bring with ourselves to the reading of the text. In other words, we misunderstand Scripture because of human ignorance, sin or error. We can refuse to hear what Scripture is teaching because we tenaciously hold onto denominational or cultural traditions or because our authority source is something other than Scripture (emotion, human reasoning).

7 THE CANON OF SCRIPTURE

The 'canon' (from a Greek word meaning a 'rule' or 'measuring stick') means the list or collection of books inspired by God and accepted as 'measuring up' as part of Scripture. This is an important issue: if we cannot determine which books belong in the Bible we will not be sure whether to believe or obey their words. The Roman Catholic Church and Orthodox Church add the Apocrypha to the Old Testament, rejected by Jews and Protestants, who only accept the standard Old Testament as inspired. Liberal critics accuse early Christians of suppressing certain 'gospels' from the NT canon. Roman Catholics argue that because the Church decided which books were to be included in the Bible, therefore the Church is the ultimate authority for our faith, not the Bible itself. How do we know which books belong in the Bible?

The answer may be illustrated by cream and milk. Cream is different to milk for three reasons: (1) a chemical difference (higher fat content), (2) a physical difference (cream floats to the top), and (3) a taste difference. But the last two differences arise from the first, chemical difference. Similarly, books that were divinely-inspired (intrinsically different) produced two other results, a different 'taste' reaction in readers and, over time, a clear line of separation between books accepted as inspired and those not inspired. There are three factors involved in canonicity:

Divine Inspiration: God is the One who determined which books would be included in the Bible by inspiring them. God gave us the Bible, not the church, because divine inspiration determined canonicity, not the Church's authority. Those books which are not inspired give themselves away with absurd or banal statements or doctrinal aberrations, nor do they have the life-changing power of inspired books.

Christ's Authority: Christ and His teachings are the test of biblical canonicity. Thus, Jesus broadly outlined the contents of the OT by speaking about its three main divisions: 'the Law, the Prophets and the Psalms' (Luke 24:44). He further clearly affirmed the limits of the Old Testament canon by telling us its first and last books: 'from the blood of

Abel to the blood of Zechariah' (Matthew 23:35 and Luke 1:51), Abel being the first martyr of the OT (in Genesis) and Zechariah the last martyr of the OT (in 2 Chronicles 24:20-21), as the Hebrew Bible has the same books as our OT, but in a different order which finishes with 2 Chronicles. F. F. Bruce writes, 'No body of literature ever had its credentials confirmed by a higher authority'[10].

Christ also pre-authenticated (that is, predicted and gave His authority to) the NT writings. Thus, he spoke about the three great divisions of the NT: the historical books ('the Holy Spirit will bring ... to your remembrance all things that I said to you', John 14:26), the doctrinal books ('He will teach you all things, John 14:26) and the prophetical books ('He will tell you things to come', John 16:13). Christ Himself is the test by which we judge whether a book belongs in the NT canon: (a) Was it written by one of Christ's apostles or one who had close connections with them (e.g. Luke 1:2), and therefore a reliable historical witness of His life in the gospels, or one whom Christ called to be His representative (see Luke 10:16, John 13:20)? (b) Is its content focused upon Christ and its truth in harmony with what we learn of Christ elsewhere? Christ's apostles also authenticate each others' writings as Scripture alongside the OT in 1 Timothy 5:18 (which quotes Deuteronomy 25:4 and Luke 10:7 and calls them both 'Scripture') and 2 Peter 3:16 (where Peter calls Paul's writings 'Scripture').

The Holy Spirit's Witness: The Holy Spirit's worldwide work in the hearts of believers resulted in the reception of the canon, because the books spoke with God's authority and life-changing power, told about God's plan of salvation and accorded with the truths found in other books in the Bible. On the other hand, various OT apocryphal books contain unbiblical teachings (salvation by works, prayers for the dead, purgatory, etc.) which contradict the revelation found in the canonical books. B. M. Metzger writes, 'The canon was not the result of a series of contests involving church politics ... When the pronouncement was made about the canon, it merely ratified what the general sensitivity of the church had already determined.... The canon is a list of authoritative books more than it is an authoritative list of books'[11].

Section Two:

The Doctrine of God

8 TEN REASONS FOR BELIEVING IN GOD

1. **Creation** (Gen. 1:1, Ps. 19:1, 33:6, 100:3, Isa. 40:26, Rom. 1:19-20). The idea that the universe sprang into existence from nothing, for no reason, in an instant of time, defies common sense. 'An atheist is someone who believes that nothing made everything' (Ray Comfort). This is like the joke about the Big Bang: first there was nothing, then it exploded. Houses do not build themselves; they require a builder (Heb. 3:4). So too, the cosmos requires a Creator.

2. **Design** (Ps. 104:24, 111:2, 139:14, Prov. 3:19, Jer. 10:12). Design in nature shows that there is an Intelligent Maker behind it. Biological wonders abound in nature: sight, flight, and reproduction for starters. Socrates (c. 469-399 BC) argued for design because of 'the position of our eyes and nose directly above our mouth to prevent that which is unacceptable for consumption'. The Universe is 'finely-tuned' for life: numerous physical forces (e.g. electromagnetic, gravitational) have to be 'just right' for life to exist, and the probability of this happening by chance is vanishingly small. Sir Fred Hoyle wrote, 'a super intellect has monkeyed with physics, as well as with chemistry and biology'[12].

3. **Conscience** (John 8:9, Romans 2:14-15, 13:5, 1 Tim. 1:5, Heb. 9:14). Conscience is a voice placed within us by God that gives us a sense of right and wrong. C. S. Lewis wrote, 'human beings, all over the earth, have this curious idea that they ought to behave in a certain way, and cannot really get rid of it. [But] they do not in fact behave in that way. They know the Law of Nature; they break it'[13]. We have a strong sense of right and wrong, however atoms do not hate, hurricanes do not forgive, nor are there any moral laws among animals. We are not merely animals or matter – our moral sense points to moral laws, and a Lawgiver.

4. **Providence** (Neh. 9:6, Psalm 36:6, 68:19, 136:25, Matt. 5:45, Acts 17:25, 1 Tim. 6:17, Heb. 1:3, Col. 1:17). The word providence means God's faithful care for His creation. Psalm 145:9 says 'His tender mercies are over all His works'. There are about 400 billion birds in the world, and none fall to the ground apart from God's will (Matt. 10:29). God's

active care over His Creation is a witness to His existence. Acts 14:17 says 'He did not leave Himself without witness, in that He did good, gave us rain from heaven and fruitful seasons'.

5. **Culture:** Virtually every human culture has been religious, and the majority of people on earth believe in God. Theologians call this the *'sensus divinitatis'*. Cicero asked, 'What people is there or what race of men, which has not some traditional teaching, some presentiment of the existence of God?' Augustine wrote, 'A sense of Deity is inscribed on every heart. Nay, even idolatry is ample evidence of this fact'.

6. **Miracles** (Ps. 78:43, Acts 2:22, Rom. 1:3-4, Heb. 2:3-4). God worked miracles throughout Biblical history as confirmation of the message His prophets delivered. The ultimate miracle (the resurrection) declares that Jesus Christ was God's Son, and is thus the ultimate proof of God's existence.

7. **History:** God's hand is seen in human history, particularly of Israel and the church. What explains the continued existence of Israel other than God, or the start of the Christian church except the resurrection?

8. **Scripture** (Psalm 19:7-11, Heb. 1:1). We find out more about God from the Bible than we do from creation, just like we find out more about a man by talking to him than by looking at a house he has built. In Scripture, God has revealed Himself to us through the medium of language, through men's words inspired by His Spirit. The divine origin of the Bible is seen in its permanence, popularity, unity, fulfilled prophecy, Christ's testimony and its life-changing power.

9. **Christ** (John 1:1, 14, 18, 20:28, Heb. 1:1-3, 1 Pet. 1:20-21). The primary reason we believe in God is because He has revealed Himself in Christ, and demonstrated this by His resurrection.

10. **Conversion** (Acts 2:38, Eph. 2:1, 1 Thess. 1:9-10). God invites us each one to come to know Him personally: 'O, taste and see that the Lord is good, blessed is the man who trusts in Him' (Ps. 34:8).

9 WHO IS GOD?

There are many false gods (1 Cor. 8:5-6) and false ideas about God:

Polytheism: There are many gods. But the unity of creation (uniform laws, atomic structure, DNA in all living things) suggests one Creator.
Pantheism: God is found in all of creation, and is one with creation. But the wisdom seen in creation argues for an Intelligent, Personal, Creator.
Deism: There is a God, but He does not intervene in His Universe. This is a denial of God's power and love to care for His creation.
Atheism: A denial of God's existence. However, since it is impossible to know for certain that God does not exist, atheism is really only ...
Agnosticism: a denial that we can know whether God exists. But honest, open-minded Agnosticism cannot deny the possibility of knowing God.

THE TRUE AND LIVING GOD

In Jeremiah 10, God is compared to the false-gods of the nations. By contrast to man-made idols, Jeremiah describes the True God: He is Great (v6 – You are great, and Your name is great in might), Unique (v7 – there is none like You), True (v10 – But the Lord is the true God), Living (v10 – He is the living God), Eternal (v10 – and the everlasting King), the God of wrath (v10 – At His wrath the earth shall tremble), Power (v12 – He has made the earth by His power), and Wisdom (v12 – He has established the world by His wisdom), He upholds Creation (see v13), He belongs to us (v16a – He is the Portion of Jacob), and we belong to Him (v16b – Israel is the tribe of His inheritance).

DEFINING GOD

Some people object to the idea of defining God by saying that we thereby confine God by our words. If the heaven of heavens cannot contain Him (1 Kings 8:27), how then can we define God? However the world is full of false ideas about God, and for this reason it is important that we properly understand and explain who God is by describing His Being and defining His attributes. Here are some definitions of God:
- 'God is an invisible, personal and living Spirit, distinguished from all other spirits by several kinds of attributes: metaphysically God is self-

existent, eternal, and unchanging; intellectually God is omniscient, faithful and wise; ethically God is just, merciful, and loving; emotionally God detests evil, is longsuffering, and is compassionate; existentially God is free, authentic, and omnipotent; relationally God is transcendent in being, immanent universally in providential activity, and immanent with His people in redemptive activity' (G. R. Lewis[14]).

- God is 'a Personal Being, Infinite in Holiness, Power, Wisdom and Goodness, Self-existent and Self-sufficient, Who in His Essence is Spirit, Light, and Love, the Great Source, Author, and Sustainer of all things' (W. Hoste[15]).

Definition: We shall define God as the Personal, Spiritual, Eternal Being, Perfect in Power, Intellect and Morality. We will therefore consider God's attributes under seven broad areas: existence, spirituality, personality, intellect, morality, sovereignty and perfection.

GOD'S ATTRIBUTES

The attempt to divide God's attributes into different categories (e.g. absolute and relative, communicable and incommunicable, His nature and His character) is difficult, because all His attributes are interconnected. The Scriptures speak of God's attributes together (e.g. His 'eternal power', Rom. 1:20, His 'great love', Eph. 2:4, His enduring mercy, Ps. 136). God cannot be omnipotent if He is not also omnipresent and omniscient. God is One, and is not divisible into parts. Some list God's attributes arbitrarily (e.g., alphabetically), however the attributes are related to each other (e.g. love and mercy are moral attributes). The connection of the attributes argues against listing them arbitrarily. Some attributes also seem to stand opposed to others, e.g. God's unity is the seeming opposite of His trinity, His transcendance of His immanence, His justice of His love. These are antitheses or paradoxes, apparently contradictory statements, yet in God they are nevertheless true, united, and balanced. We struggle to understand how God is able to combine and unite the seeming opposite attributes. We must realise that God is unfathomable, far greater than the human mind can comprehend. As we shall see, this too is one of God's attributes.

10 GOD'S ATTRIBUTES: ETERNAL

God is called the Living God over thirty times in the Bible. 'He is the true God and eternal life' (1 John 5:20), the 'I AM', the eternally existing Being (Ex. 3:14). God is the One 'who is, and who was and who is to come' (Rev. 1:4). Jesus said, 'the Father has life in himself' (John 5:26).

GOD IS ETERNAL

God was not created, nor ever had a beginning, nor will He ever cease to exist. Ps. 90:2 says, 'Before the mountains were brought forth, or ever You had formed the earth and the world, even from everlasting to everlasting, You are God'. See also Gen. 21:33, Deut. 33:27, Isa. 40:28, 57:15, Jer. 10:10, Rom. 1:20 and 1 Tim. 1:17.

- **Problem**: Many people find it hard to understand how God can be eternal, and ask, Who made God? However, if God was made by something or someone, He would not be God. Either the universe is eternal (it is not), or it resulted from an infinite chain of causes (which is illogical), or it had a beginning. That is, it had a First Cause, itself uncaused – i.e. an eternal Creator.

GOD IS SELF-EXISTENT

God does not owe His existence to anyone or anything else, for He has always existed and will always exist. He was not created or caused by anything else. John 5:26 says, 'For as the Father has life in Himself, so He has granted the Son to have life in Himself'. Ps. 36:9 says, 'with You is the fountain of life and in Your light we see light'. Because God is self-existent, He is also **Self-sufficient**. God does not need food or drink for His existence like we do, or sleep to refresh Him (Ps. 121:4, Isa. 40:28), nor is there anything else that He needs supplied to Him. See Acts 17:24-25, Rom. 11:35-36, and Psalm 50:7-12.

- **Problem**: If God is self-sufficient and content in Himself, why did He create the Universe, and why did He create man? Does this not suggest that God needed something? God is a Trinity, eternally existing in a relationship of perfect fellowship between the Father, the Son and the Spirit before the creation of the world (see John 1:1, 17:5, 24). God did not create us because He lacked something which we could supply. Rather, He created us out of the abundance of His great love, so that by His grace we would be added to that Divine fellowship of the Father, Son and Holy Spirit, and enjoy and glorify God forever (1 John 1:3).

GOD IS UNCHANGING

Because God is eternal and self-sufficient, time does not change Him, nor do any of His attributes alter. Another word sometimes used for this attribute is **Immutable**. See Ps. 102:25-27, Mal. 3:6, Jam. 1:17. The fact that God is unchanging is very reassuring. If God could change, our confidence in Him would be destroyed. We could no longer be sure that He still exists, or that He loves us and cares for us. We could not trust His promises relating to salvation, or answered prayer, or Christ's return. While human love can grow stronger or cooler, God's love for us is an 'everlasting love' (Jer. 31:3). 'His love is a constant force, not a fitful emotion' (T. C. Hammond[16]). His 'eternal power' (Rom. 1:20) is not diminished from His 'wonders of old' (Ps. 77:11), His 'everlasting mercy' will never be exhausted (Ps. 100:5, 103:17), He will never deviate from His standards of 'everlasting righteousness' (Ps. 119:142). His Word is 'settled forever in heaven' (Ps. 119:89); it 'stands forever' (Isa. 40:8). His is an 'everlasting kingdom' (Ps. 145:13), an 'everlasting salvation' (Isa. 45:17), and an 'everlasting covenant' (Heb. 13:20). 'This God is our God forever and ever' (Ps. 48:14, KJV).

- **Problem**: Does not God change His mind in the Bible? For example, (a) in Gen. 6, God was sorry He had made man and decided to flood the world, (b) in Ex. 32, Moses prayed, and God promised not to destroy Israel, (c) in Jonah 3, God spared Nineveh after they repented. God always remains true to His principles of justice and mercy. When (a) people sin, God must judge, but (b) when someone intercedes or (c) people repent, God in mercy spares them. God's warnings are conditional (Jer. 18:1-10, Ezek. 33:11). While God is unchanging, He is also personal and relational. He interacts with people throughout the changing circumstances of history. God is also sovereign and free, and able to respond when people change (for good or ill).

11 GOD'S ATTRIBUTES: ALL-POWERFUL

God's power is seen in creation. Because God is the eternal Creator, He is also the Supreme Being, Lord of all. In Rom. 1:20, God's attributes of eternity and power are followed by His attribute of 'Godhead' or 'Deity', which means that He is the Supreme Being. The Bible introduces God to us in the first verse as the Creator. This is how most people come to realise that God must exist – as the Supreme Being who created us.

GOD IS SOVEREIGN

A sovereign is a supreme ruler; God's sovereignty means that He is the Lord over all things. The old Irish hymn 'Be Thou My Vision' puts it well when it adores God as the 'High King of heaven ... O ruler of all'. God is sovereign for four reasons:

1. God is sovereign because He is the eternal Creator of all things (Psalm 29:10, 93:1-2).
2. God is supreme because no one has greater power than He (Ps. 95:3, 2 Chron. 20:6).
3. God is Lord because He owns all things (Gen. 14:19, Matt. 11:25, 1 Chron. 29:11-12).
4. God is ruler because He continues to uphold and control all things in Creation (Rev. 4:2; not even a sparrow falls to the ground without His permission, Matt. 10:29).

God is in control of all things: Nations and History (Dan. 4:17, Dan. 2:21, Eph. 1:11, 3:15, Isa. 46:10; Joseph, Esther), our lives and times (our times, Ps. 31:15; breath, Dan. 5:23, events, Pr. 16:33, Rom. 8:28), salvation (God's sovereign choice, Eph. 1:4, 1 Thess. 1:4, 2 Thess. 2:13, 1 Peter 1:2, and man's free will, Deut. 30:19, Joshua 24:15, 1 Kings 18:21, Prov. 1:29, are both affirmed).

- **Problem**: How can God be sovereign when mankind (and demons) rebel against Him and disobey, when evil seems to triumph, and sin reigns through death (Rom. 5:21)? This is a mystery, but the Bible still says God reigns and is in control, even though He has given us free will.

GOD IS OMNIPOTENT

God has 'all power'; nothing is too hard for Him. He is 'Almighty God' (Gen. 17:1), the 'Lord God Omnipotent' (Rev. 19:6). 'Great is our Lord, and mighty in power' (Psalm 147:5), see also Jer. 32:27, Matt. 19:26. God's omnipotence is seen in creation: He created all things from nothing, simply by speaking the word (see Ps. 33:9, Jer. 32:17). God's omnipotence is seen in history through miracles in the OT, and in Jesus' ministry in the NT. But, there are **Things God cannot do**:

- God cannot go against His holy character (see Ps. 5:4). He cannot lie (Heb. 6:18, Tit. 1:2, Num. 23:19), be tempted by evil (Jam. 1:13), or remember our forgiven sins (see Isa 43:25).
- God cannot do logically absurd things: e.g., make a square circle, or a make a rock so large He cannot lift it, or eat Himself for breakfast (A. C. Grayling). 'Can a mortal man ask questions which God finds unanswerable? Quite easily, I should think. All nonsense questions are unanswerable' (C.S.Lewis[17]).

GOD IS TRANSCENDENT

God is far above the material universe and excels all created things. He is 'the Most High God' (Acts 16:17). 1 Kings 8:27 says 'But will God indeed dwell on the earth? Behold, heaven and the heaven of heavens cannot contain You'. See also Ps. 97:9, and 99:2.

Two Errors: Some deny God's transcendence, and teach the error of Pantheism (e.g. Hinduism, New Age spirituality) which identifies God with His creation, arguing that all creation is divine, and denies God's personality. Because all events, good or evil, are manifestations of God, evil ceases to be evil, nor is God good. Secondly, Deism teaches that God is remote and does not act in His creation or take any interest in it. He is the Divine Watchmaker, who wound up the Universe, and thereafter let it run its course. Deism denies God's immanence (He is near us, He knows us and cares for His Creation). Deists deny that God has revealed Himself in Scripture, or in the history of the world, or that He answers prayer. The Bible counters these two errors by speaking of God's transcendence alongside His immanence (see Isa 66:1-2 and Ps 8:1-4).

12 GOD'S ATTRIBUTES: SPIRITUAL

GOD IS SPIRIT

'God is Spirit' (John 4:24). By spirit, we mean that God is immaterial and intangible. He does not have a body, nor is He made of matter or energy, nor does He have measurements. 2 Cor. 3:17 says, 'Now the Lord is the Spirit; and where the Spirit of the Lord is, there is liberty'. God is called 'the Father of spirits' (Heb. 12:9).

Being spirit, God does not have a physical body. Mormons deny this, and instead teach that God is an ascended, exalted human being who once lived on earth and does have a body. Mormons point to verses which speak of the Lord's 'eyes and ears' (Ps. 34:15-16) or 'hands' (Isa. 65:2). However, God does not have a body, any more than verses which speak of God covering us with his wings and feathers (e.g. Psalm 91:4) prove that God is a bird, or verses likening God to a rock (e.g. 2 Sam. 22:32) mean that He is made of minerals, or verses comparing God to the sun (e.g. Psalm 84:11) mean that God is a blazing ball of gas. These are all word-pictures and figures of speech.

GOD IS INVISIBLE

We cannot see God, although He also chose on certain occasions in the Bible to reveal Himself visibly to various people. God is 'the King, eternal, immortal, invisible' (1 Tim. 1:17), the 'invisible God' (Col. 1:15). See also Rom. 1:20, John 1:18, Job 9:11, and also Job 23:8, 9.

Some people find it hard to believe in a God they cannot see. However, if God were physical or visible, He would be no different to nature or creation, and therefore He would not be God at all. Many people and cultures throughout history have worshipped 'creation rather than the Creator' (Rom. 1:25, Deut. 4:19, 2 Kings 23:5, Jer. 8:2, Rom. 1:23). Many people and cultures have worshipped idols, that is, visible images or representations of a deity (Acts 17:16). Many of the most beautiful descriptions of God are found in passages showing the foolishness and emptiness of idolatry (e.g., Jeremiah 10).

- **Problem**: If God is invisible, how is it that we read about certain people in the Bible seeing God? See, for example, Exodus 24:9-11, 33:18, Isa. 6:1-5, Eze. 1:26-28 and Rev. 4:3. Because God is a spirit, and thus is intrinsically invisible, the reason that God appears to certain people in the Bible is because God chooses to reveal Himself for certain purposes. If someone asks, How is it possible for the invisible God to become visible, the answer is simply because God is able to do anything He pleases, provided it is in accordance with His sovereign will and holy character.

GOD IS OMNIPRESENT

God is present everywhere, although He is also able to presence Himself in certain locations. Psalm 139:7-10 describes the impossibility of escaping from God's presence. See also Jer. 23: 24. God is not limited to Heaven, let alone an earthly building (1 Kings 8:27, Acts 17:24). Instead, we can worship God anywhere (John 4:21-24). On the other hand, in the Bible we find God described as present in certain locations. 'God is in heaven' (Ps. 115:3, Ecc. 5:20); and He met with His people at the Tabernacle (Ex. 25:22, 30:6). Thus, even though God is present in certain places, He is also present everywhere. Here is another mystery about God beyond our finite understanding. Another way of describing God's omnipresence is to say that God is **Immanent**. That is, God pervades the universe, and more than this, God is near to us. He is a 'God near at hand' (Jer. 23:23). He is not 'a God away out there, who doesn't care'. See also Acts 17:26-28, Deut. 4:7 and Ps. 46:1, 7.

Balance: God is thus both the transcendent sovereign Lord and the immanent helper near at hand. We need to hold both truths in tension. He is the Most High God, yet in grace He condescends to consider us (Ps. 113:4-7). It is necessary to remind ourselves of God's transcendence so that we do not treat God with a casual or crass familiarity. It is also important to trust in God's immanence, believing that He is 'near to all who call upon Him, to all who call upon Him in truth … He also will hear their cry and save them' (Ps 145:18-19).

13 GOD'S ATTRIBUTES: PERSONAL

Although God is Spirit, and thus immaterial, yet He is also a Person, and thus very much like us. God is not a force, nor a concept, nor a law of nature, nor Love, nor 'the soul of the Universe'. God is not simply 'the Ground of Being'. God is not 'an Infinite and Eternal Energy, from which all things proceed'. God is not an 'It' at all – He is a He. Because God is the Living God, He possesses all the characteristics of personality that non-living and impersonal things lack.

GOD POSSESSES A WILL

God has wishes, desires, purposes and plans; He has the ability to make choices and decisions, see Eph. 1:5, 1:11, 3:11, Psalm 135:6. In particular, it was God's purpose and will that His Son, Jesus Christ, should die for our sins (Acts 2:23, 4:28). It is God's purpose that His kingdom will come on earth; we pray, 'Your kingdom come. Your will be done on earth as it is in heaven' (Matt. 6:10). As the Sovereign and all-powerful Lord, God is **Free**, and does whatever He wishes. He is not constrained by any external force other than His own desire. His will is therefore perfect, for there are none of the compromises with God that we are forced to make in our decisions. See Ps. 115:3, Dan. 4:35. The fact that God has a will – that He makes decisions, that He chooses certain things, and that He acts, reacts and interacts – all this means that God is not a static Being, a passive and unmoving 'It', a remote and impersonal Deity. The attribute of God's will therefore presents a contrast with the fact that God is eternal and unchanging and must be balanced against it.

GOD POSSESSES EMOTIONS

God has feelings or sentiments. Emotion in itself is not an ignoble thing, and this is proved when we look at God. God is not an austere Majesty who gives an expressionless response to every situation. God's words reveal more than cold, remorseless reason or inescapable logic. He is the Living God, whose personality shows itself by expression of deep feelings. God laughs (Ps. 2:4), rejoices (Zeph. 3:17), is astonished or amazed (Isaiah 59:16) or grieved (Psalm 95:10), He can be saddened (Genesis 6:6), but 'in His presence is fullness of joy' (Psalm 16:11). God is **Jealous** when His people commit spiritual adultery (Ex. 20:5, Deut. 4:24, 5:9, 6:15, 32:16, 21, Josh. 24:19, Ezek. 23:25, 36:5, Nah. 1:2). The Bible teaches us about God's **Anger** (see Ps. 7:11, Ex. 4:14, Num. 25:4, John 3:36, Rom. 1:18) or wrath (which can occur without sin, Eph. 4:26, Matt. 5:22). We may be sure that God's anger is not a fit of temper. See also Jer. 10:10, Rom. 1:18, and Col. 3:6. God is **Longsuffering** (see Num. 14:18, Ps. 86:15, Neh. 9:17). Being longsuffering is the opposite of anger. While God is angry because of our sins, yet He restrains Himself and withholds punishment.

- **Impassibility**? Some argue that God does not have passions, emotions or feelings, nor does God ever suffer. However, the evidence we have seen calls into question the 'impassibility of God', for God clearly does have emotions and responds to events in ways that involve emotion. God is not the austere, remote, impersonal Unmoved Mover of Greek philosophy – He is the Living God.

GOD IS RELATIONAL

God is interpersonal; He has revealed Himself to us so that we can know Him and be friends of God, like Abraham. It is because God is personal that He has names. Above all, as our Lord Jesus Christ taught us, we have come to know God as Father. For God to be love means that He must have relationships, and being eternal, that He must have eternal relationships that pre-existed Creation, relationships within His own Being, hence the idea of the Trinity. God is Tri-personal. God's emotions are part of what constitute God a relational Being – they are the outward expressions of His inward feelings. But if God were not relational, He could just commune with Himself in His own heart. Instead, God's emotional attributes respond to other persons and situations. God's pleasure and delight was expressed publicly in response to Christ's perfect life at His baptism, just as God's wrath is reserved for His enemies (Nah. 1:2). As a relational Being, God communicates and reveals Himself and His truth to His creatures.

14 GOD'S ATTRIBUTES: ALL-KNOWING

God has a mind (see 1 Cor. 2:16 and Rom. 11:34). He thinks (see Ps. 92:5, Isa. 55:8-9 and Jer. 29:11) and He thinks about us (see Psalm 40:5, 17, 139:17). The reason why we think is because we are made in God's image. God has given us mental faculties, above all so that we might know Him. The Bible speaks of three main types of mental ability: knowledge, understanding and wisdom. Knowledge is the acquisition of facts and information. Understanding involves intelligence and thinking. Wisdom is the highest of the three, and is the practical application of knowledge and the prudent use of intelligence. These three faculties go together in the Bible (e.g. Ex. 31:3, 35:31, Isa. 11:2 and Col. 1:9).

GOD IS OMNISCIENT

God knows all things: the number of stars (Ps. 147:4) and their names (Isa. 40:26), the number of hairs on our heads (Matt. 10:30), our words and thoughts (Ps. 139:1-4), 'the hearts of all the sons of men' (1 Kings 8:39, Prov. 15:11, 1 John 3:20, and see Heb. 4:13), and our needs before we ask (Matt. 6:8). He 'counts all my steps' (Job 31:4); 'You number my wanderings; Put my tears into Your bottle; Are they not in Your book?' (Ps. 56:8). God knows the future: 'He knows the way that I take' (Job 23:10). He knows 'the end from the begining' (Isa. 46:10). God knows the day of Christ's return (Matt. 24:36). God's omniscience leaves us overwhelmed (Ps. 139:6):

- God is able to hear the prayers of people all over the world all praying at the same time
- God hears all the words that everybody on earth is saying at the same time, and through all time.
- God hears and knows all the thoughts of everybody on earth.

'God knows instantly and effortlessly all matter and all matters, all mind and every mind ... all mysteries, all enigmas, all feeling, all desires, every unuttered secret ... all things visible and invisible in heaven and in earth, motion, space, time, life, death, good, evil, heaven, and hell' (Tozer[18]).

God Has Infinite Understanding

God has perfect intelligence. Ps. 147:5 says, 'Great is our Lord, and mighty in power; His understanding is infinite'. His understanding is 'unsearchable' (Isaiah 40:28). See also Job 12:13, Prov. 3:19, Jer. 10:12, 51:15. The idea of understanding goes beyond mere knowledge of facts to the faculty of thinking, intelligence, reflection and perception. We see God's infinite intelligence in **Nature:** Agur marvelled at things in nature too wonderful for him: 'the way of an eagle in the air, the way of a serpent on a rock ... and the way of man with a virgin' (Prov. 30:19). God said to Job, 'Where were you when I laid the foundations of the earth? Tell me if you have understanding' (Job 38:4). God goes on to speak about the sea, the sunrise, snow, lightning, stars, clouds, and animals (Job 38-9). **Scripture:** critics who dared to attack and accuse God's Word of error have been proved wrong time and again. Agur could write, 'Every word of God is pure, He is a shield to those tho put their trust in Him. Do not add to His words, lest He rebuke you, and you be found a liar' (Prov. 30:5-6).

God Is All-Wise

God's ways and plans are the best (Isa. 55:9). He is 'the only wise God' (Rom. 16:27). God is nowhere described in the Bible as 'all-wise'. However, in Christ are 'hidden all the treasures of wisdom and knowledge' (Col. 2:3) and the believer may possess 'all wisdom' through prayer (Col. 1:9) and the Word of Christ (Col. 3:16). Therefore, as wisdom comes from God (Prov. 2:6, Jam. 1:5), all wisdom must belong to Him; see also Rom. 11:33. Wisdom is more than knowledge; it is the right use of knowledge, is practical, and attained through experience (see Job 12:12). Wisdom has a moral and spiritual element to it: living the right way morally, treating other people properly and fairly, fearing God (Ps. 111:10, Prov. 9:10), and living before Him humbly and obediently. God's wisdom is seen in: **Creation.** See Ps. 104:24, 136:5, Jer. 51:15 and Prov. 3:19. **Salvation.** See 1 Cor. 1:22-24, and 30 (Christ has become for us 'wisdom from God'). **His Plans for Our lives:** 'As for God, His way is perfect ... [He] makes my way perfect' (Ps. 18:30, 32). 'All things work together for good to those who love God' (Rom. 8:28).

15 GOD'S ATTRIBUTES: HOLY

Perhaps the most glorious of God's attributes are His moral attributes. We see this when Moses asked God to show him His glory. God described Himself as 'The LORD, the LORD God, merciful and gracious, longsuffering and abounding in goodness and truth, keeping mercy for thousands, forgiving iniquity and transgression and sin, by no means clearing the guilty, visiting the iniquity of the fathers upon the children and the children's children to the third and fourth generation' (Ex. 34:6-7).

GOD IS HOLY

The word 'holy' means 'set apart' and means that God is (a) separate and distinct from anything else, unique and perfect, and (b) separate from anything impure or sinful, characterized by absolute moral perfection. Isaiah calls God 'the Holy One' 27 times, most famously in Isaiah 6, where the seraphim cry, 'Holy, holy, holy is the LORD of hosts; the whole earth is full of His glory' (Isaiah 6:3). Moses praised God in Exodus 15:11 with these words: 'Who is like You, O LORD, among the gods? Who is like You, glorious in holiness, fearful in praises, doing wonders?' Hannah said, 'No one is holy like the LORD, for there is none besides You, nor is there any rock like our God' (1 Sam. 2:2). God is called 'the Holy One' (Job 6:10), 'the Holy One of Israel' (Isaiah 1:4); He says, 'I the Lord your God am holy' (Lev. 11:44-45, 19:2, 20:7, 26, 21:8, etc), and speaks of 'My holy name' (Lev. 20:3, 22:32, and see Isa. 57:15).

Habakkuk 1:12 says 'O LORD my God, my Holy One', but verse 13 goes on to say, 'You are of purer eyes than to behold evil, and cannot look upon wickedness'. James 1:13 says, 'God cannot be tempted by evil'. Israel was told: 'be holy, for I the LORD your God am holy' (Lev. 19:2, a command repeated to Christians in the New Testament in 1 Peter 1:16). In its OT context, this involved commands like 'Do not turn to idols' (Lev. 19:4), nor steal (Lev. 19:11), and 'you shall not curse the deaf' (Lev. 19:14). Being holy means separation from evil and all that is contrary to God's character.

GOD IS RIGHTEOUS

God's righteousness means that He is totally fair, impartial, truthful and faithful. If God's holiness speaks negatively of God's separation from sin, God's righteousness speaks positively of the fact that God always does what is right. See Deut. 32:3-4, Psalm 89:14. Psalm 11:7 says, 'For the LORD is righteous, He loves righteousness; His countenance beholds the upright'. 'The Lord loves righteousness' means that He hates what is not righteous.

One of God's descriptions in the Bible is that He is a **Judge** who always does what is right (see Gen. 18:25). Indeed, the word 'just' (from which we get 'justice', 'judge' and 'judgment') is the same word in the Bible as 'righteous'. Because God is righteous, He is also the 'God of **truth**' (Deut. 32:4), for God cannot lie (Titus 1:2, Num. 23:19). Psalm 31:5 calls him the 'LORD God of truth' (see also Isaiah 65:16). 'Every word of God is pure' (Proverbs 30:5). God's Word is truth (John 17:17). God is also **Faithful**: He keeps His Word and His promises. See Psalm 145:13(b), Deut. 7:9, Lam. 3:23 ('great is Your faithfulness'). The NT reassures us three times that 'God is faithful' (1 Cor. 1:9, 1 Cor. 10:13, 2 Cor. 1:18). Notice that all three of these promises of God's faithfulness were written to the Corinthians, perhaps the least faithful and most sinful of all the churches we find in the NT.

As a God of righteousness, God cannot overlook sin, and as a God of justice, God must punish sin. Yet despite the fact that 'all have sinned' (Rom. 3:23), we can be 'justified (pronounced righteous) freely through the redemption that is in Christ Jesus, whom God set forth as a propitiation' (Rom. 3:24-25). What this means is that, in our Lord Jesus' death, a ransom-price has been paid, a righteous basis for showing sinners mercy has been established, and that God can pronounce those who believe in Christ perfectly righteous in His sight. God has found a way to be 'just and the justifier of the one who has faith in Jesus' (Rom. 3:26).

16 GOD'S ATTRIBUTES: LOVING

Love means seeking and doing what is best for others, even at one's own expense. God's love is the most wonderful of God's attributes. If God's holiness is negative, in that God is separate from sin, and God's righteousness is, in a sense neutral, in that God is always just and upright (or, in Hebrew, 'straight'), giving people no more or no less than they deserve, we could say that God's love goes beyond these two attributes and is positively overflowing with blessings.

The Bible tells us that God is Love (1 John 4:8). Ephesians 2:4 tells us that God's love for us is great: 'being rich in mercy, because of His great love with which He loved us'. John 3:16 says, 'For God so loved the world that He gave His only begotten Son, that whoever believes in Him should not perish but have everlasting life'.

Other words which teach us similar truths about God include good, gracious and merciful. The Lord is **Good**; that is, He is kind. God alone is good (Luke 18:19). The Bible repeatedly tells us that 'the LORD is good' (Ps. 100:5, 106:1, 145:9, Jer. 33:11). Psalm 33:5 says 'the earth is full of the goodness of the LORD'. Psalm 119:68 says 'You are good, and do good'. Psalm 34:8 says, 'Oh, taste and see that the LORD is good; blessed is the man who trusts in Him!'

The Lord is **Gracious**; that is, He freely gives us far more than what we deserve. He is 'the God of all grace' (1 Peter 5:10). Psalm 145:8 says, 'The LORD is gracious and full of compassion, slow to anger and great in mercy'. See also Neh. 9:17, Joel 2:13. Ephesians 1:7 says, 'In Him we have redemption through His blood, the forgiveness of sins, according to the riches of His grace'. Ephesians 2:7 says that, having been saved, 'in the ages to come He might show the exceeding riches of His grace towards us in Christ Jesus'. See also Rom. 3:24 and Eph. 2:8.

The Lord is **Merciful**; that is, He is compassionate and takes pity on the needy or those in distress. See Ex. 34:6-7, 2 Sam. 24:14, Ps. 86:15,

103:8. Psalm 5:7 speaks of the 'multitude of Your mercy'. Ephesians 2:4 speaks about God being 'rich in mercy'.

- **Problem**: If God is loving and good, why is there evil and suffering in the world? The question implies that evil is real, but for the atheist, the universe is materialistic, not moral, and there is no such thing as good or evil. Our sense of right and wrong is real, however, and points to transcendent laws of morality that themselves point to a Lawgiver.

THE GREATNESS OF GOD'S LOVE

In Ephesians 3:18-19, Paul prays that the Ephesian Christians may be able to understand the love of God in all its dimensions: width and length and depth and height – to 'know the love of Christ which passes knowledge, that you may be filled with all the fullness of God'. John 3:16 helps us to understand just how great God's love is.

1. It tells us firstly about the height of God's love. He is the Most High God, creator of Heaven and earth, and we are so insignificant, it is amazing God should love us. In addition, God is holy and perfect, yet He loves us despite the fact that we are guilty and disobedient, sinners (Rom. 5:8) and His enemies (5:10). 1 John 4:10 says, 'In this is love, not that we loved God, but that He loved us'. The Lord Jesus was 'the friend of sinners' (Matt. 11:19).
2. The breadth of God's love is amazing. John 3:16 tells us that God so loved the world. God loves all people, of all races, of all social classes, the rich and poor, the important and the smallest people are no different to him. John 3:16 reminds us that '*whoever* believes in Him shall not perish but have everlasting life'.
3. The depth of God's love is amazing. Out of love, He sent His Son to death on the Cross (Phil. 2:5-8). 1 John 4:9 says, 'In this the love of God was manifested toward us, that God has sent His only begotten Son into the world, that we might live through Him'.
4. The length of God's love is amazing. God's love goes on forever: whoever believes in Him shall not perish but have everlasting life. God says, 'I have loved you with an everlasting love' (Jer. 31:3). Romans 8:39 reminds us that nothing will be able to separate us from the love of God in Christ Jesus our Lord.

17 GOD'S ATTRIBUTES: PERFECT

GOD IS PERFECT

Jesus said, 'Your Father in heaven is perfect' (Matt. 5:48). God's way is perfect (Ps. 18:30), His work is perfect (Deut. 32:4), His law is perfect (Ps. 19:7), His will is perfect (Rom. 12:2), and He is perfect in knowledge (Job 37:16). All of God's attributes are possessed by Him in perfection: He has infinite understanding (Ps. 147:5), He is all-wise, all-powerful, omnipresent, perfectly righteous, faithful, true, loving and good. God would not be God if He were not a morally perfect Being. God 'is humanity raised to the nth power' (Scroggie[19]). If God exists, He must be perfect; He would not be God if He were deficient in any area – whether power or knowledge or existence. God is also perfect in His personality, whereas our personalities have their quirks and eccentricities. He is perfectly balanced in His attributes: both personal and spiritual, transcendant and immanent, unchanging and freely acting, Saviour and Judge, righteous and loving, unity and yet Trinity.

Novatian wrote: 'Here, and in all our meditations upon the qualities and content of God, we pass beyond our power of fit conception, nor can human eloquence put forth a power to commensurate with His greatness. At the contemplation and utterance of His majesty all eloquence is rightly dumb, all mental effort is feeble'.

There are other similar words used to describe God's perfection: He is **Great**. Psalm 145:3 says, 'Great is the Lord and greatly to be praised; His greatness is unsearchable' (see also 'the great God', Deut. 10:17; Ps. 95:3). He is **Unique** ('to whom will you liken Me? Isa. 40:18, 25, see also 46:5); 'Who is like You, O LORD, among the gods? Who is like You, glorious in holiness, Fearful in praises, doing wonders?' (Ex. 15:11).

GOD IS ONE

One of God's attributes is His unity. Deut. 6:4 says, 'Hear, O Israel: The LORD our God, the LORD is one!' (Mark 12:29, 1 Cor. 8: 4, 6). 1 Tim. 2:5 says, 'There is one God and one mediator between God and men, the man Christ Jesus'. He is 'the only true God' (John 17:3).

This is why it is so difficult to divide God's attributes into two or three categories. God cannot be sub-divided into parts. Instead, all of God's attributes are linked to other attributes. Think, for example, of the relation between God's omnipotence, omniscience and omnipresence. If God was not omnipresent, He would not be omnipotent, for He could not do things where He was not and if He was not omniscient, He would not be omnipotent, for 'knowledge is power'. All of God's attributes characterise each other: God's power is righteous, eternal, wise, invisible, etc.

The reason why God is a unity is that God is a Person and a Spirit. As a person, 'Everything He does is an act of the whole person' (Grudem[20]); God does not have a split personality. Nor, as Spirit, is God made up of building blocks (like we are composed of molecules, cells, organs, etc.); He would then be dependent upon other things for His existence; but He has Life in Himself. Another word sometimes used is God's **Simplicity**, meaning that God is not composed of parts. Grudem helpfully explains that God is not part 'light' and part 'love' (1 John 1:5, 4:8); we must not think that 'God is a loving God at one point in history, and a just or wrathful God at another'[21].

GOD IS GLORIOUS

God's glory is His majestic excellence displayed for all to see and honour. In Isa. 6:3, the seraphim cried, 'Holy, holy, holy is the LORD of hosts; the whole earth is full of His glory'! He is 'the King of glory' (Psalm 24:8-10), 'the God of glory' (Ps. 29:3, Acts 7:2), and 'the Father of glory' (Eph. 1:17). Christ is 'the Lord of glory (1 Cor. 2:8, James 2:1), while we read of the Spirit of glory in 1 Pet. 4:14. We are to 'give Him glory' (Rev. 19:7), however mankind 'did not glorify Him as God (Rom. 1:21).

God's perfection is **Beautiful**. Psalm 27:4, 90:17 speaks of 'the beauty of the Lord' (see also Isa. 33:17). Because of God's greatness and excellence, He (and He only) deserves to be **Worshipped**.

18 THE TRINITY

C. S. Lewis wrote that the Trinity is either the most farcical doctrine invented by the early disciples or the most profound and thrilling mystery revealed by the Creator Himself. To demonstrate the Trinity, we need to establish three facts: (1) The Father, Son and Holy Spirit are all God, (2) They are Three Distinct Persons, and yet (3) They are One God.

1. The Father, Son and Holy Spirit are all God
A. The Father is God ('God the Father', John 6:27, Gal. 1:1, Phil. 2:11, etc.). The fact that Christ prayed to, obeyed and served His Father, shows that the Father is God.

B. Christ is God (see Matt. 1:23, John 1:1, 20:28, Rom. 9:5, 2 Cor. 4:6, 5:19, Phil. 2:6, Col. 2:9, Tit. 2:13, Heb. 1:8, 2 Pet. 1:1 and Isa. 9:6). He also shares God's Attributes: **Creator** (John 1:3, 10, Col. 1:16, Heb. 1:2, 10), **Eternal** (1 John 1:1-2. Isa. 9:6), **Unchanging** (Heb. 1:11-12, 13:8), **All-Knowing** (Matt. 11:27, John 2:24, 16:30), **Omnipresent** (John 1:48, Matt. 18:20), **Forgiving Sin** (Mark 2:5-7), **Worshipped** (Heb. 1:6, Phil. 2:10), **Saviour** (1 John 4:14, cf. Isa. 45:21), **Judge** (Acts 10:42, cf. Gen. 18:25, Isa. 45:23). Christ also takes God's Names: **Jehovah** (Heb. 1:10-12, cf. Ps. 102:24-27, Mark 1:3), **I AM** (John 8:58, cf. Ex. 3:14), **Rock** (1 Cor. 10:4, cf. Sam. 2:2, Ps. 18:31), **Alpha and Omega** (Rev. 1:8, cf. Rev. 22:13). Christ is also **Equal with God** (John 5:18, 17:5, Psalm 110:1; only someone equal with God can sit alongside Him).

C. The Holy Spirit is God. He is called the 'Spirit of God' (Gen. 1:2, plus 25 refs.). See also Acts 5:3-4 and Romans 8:9. The Holy Spirit shares God's characteristics: Eternal (Heb. 9:14), Omnipresent (Psalm 139:7), Omniscient (1 Cor. 2:10-11),

2. The Father, Son and Holy Spirit are Distinct Persons
We hardly need any proof that the Father and the Son are persons; evidence that the Holy Spirit is a person (not an impersonal force) is seen in Acts 10:20 and 13:2 (He uses the word 'I' when talking), and the Holy

Spirit is also described as 'He' (not 'it') in John 14:26. The Holy Spirit also possesses personal characteristics: he speaks (Acts 8:29), has a will (1 Cor. 12:11), prays (Rom. 8:26), can be sinned against (Matt. 12:31), grieved (Eph. 4:30), insulted (Heb. 10:29), jealous (Jam. 4:5). The Father, Son and Holy Spirit are distinct persons (John 14:16, 14:26, 15:26, 16:7, 16:13-14, Rom. 8:26, 1 John 4:14). The NT places the Father, Son and Holy Spirit together in triplets, like in Matt. 28:19 (note: 'name' singular, but three names), 2 Cor. 13:14, Rev. 1:4-5.

3. The Father, Son and Spirit are One God

The Bible teaches that there is only one God (Deut. 6:4, Mark 12:32, 1 Tim. 2:5, James 2:19). It also teaches that the Father, Son and Spirit are one (John 10:30, 14:8-11, Rom. 8:9-10, 2 Cor. 3:16-18).

Old Testament Foreshadowings of the truth of the Trinity: Gen. 1:1 – 'In the beginning God (Elohim – plur.) created (sing.) the heavens and the earth', Gen. 1:26, Isa. 48:16, and Zech. 13:7.

Objections to the Doctrine of the Trinity
1. There are no references to the word Trinity in the Bible. But neither are terms like the Incarnation, or the Second Coming, or even the word 'Bible' used in the Bible. This does not make them untrue.
2. Verses describing the Son's subjection or obedience to the Father (e.g. John 14:28) indicate that the Son was a subordinate being. However, this was not because He was inferior in Person, but rather in the Position that He deliberately took, humbling himself for the purposes of redemption (Phil. 2:7-8).
3. The One God takes different forms, as Father (in the OT), as Son (in the Gospels), and as Spirit (in Acts and present day). This is the heresy of 'Modalism', disproven, for example, by Christ praying to the Father to send the Spirit (John 14:16).
4. The Trinity is a physical and mathematical impossibility. However, God is beyond physics. This is why all attempts to defend the Trinity by analogy fail, e.g. the shamrock (God is not tripartite), three states of matter (this is modalism). 'God is not like anything' (Tozer[22]).

19 GOD'S SERVANTS: ANGELS

Angels are 'God's secret agents' (Billy Graham). Angels are 'those spiritual beings which God created higher than humans, some of whom have remained obedient to God and carry out his will, and others of whom disobeyed, lost their holy condition, and now oppose and hinder his work' (Ericksen[23]).

Angels are spiritual beings of great power and dignity, created by God to serve Him. They are mentioned nearly 300 times in the Bible, from Gen. 3:24 (cherubim in the garden of Eden) to Rev. 22:16. However, we are given no systematic explanation of who angels are or in-depth treatment of what they do. The Bible teaches that we should not worship angels or try to intrude into their invisible realm (Col. 2:18). Instead we should worship God (Rev. 22:8-9) and Christ who created them (Col. 1:16).

We learn from angels that there is an invisible spiritual world beyond the visible physical world. Despite the fact that angels are immensely powerful and glorious, yet they humbly serve God and His people. The angels are like their Master – great and yet willing to serve (Mark 10:45).

WHAT ARE ANGELS?

- created beings (Col. 1:16, Neh. 9:6); we are not told when they were created (they are not mentioned during Gen. 1, but they might have been created at this time, or before the rest of creation, Job 38:7)
- spirits (Ps. 104:4, Eph. 6:12, Heb. 1:7)
- greater than humans (Heb. 2:7, 2 Pet 2:10-11)
- powerful ('who excel in strength', Ps. 103:20). One angel killed 185,000 Assyrian soldiers in one night (2 Kings 19:35)
- numerous (Heb. 12:22, Rev. 5:11, 'hosts, armies': Ps. 103:21, 148:2)
- of different ranks (principalities and powers, Col. 1:16, cf. Eph. 1:21; archangel, Dan. 10:13, seraphim, Isa. 6:2, cherubim, Ezek. 1:4)
- intelligent (Eph. 3:9-10, 1 Pet. 1:12, 2 Sam. 14:17, 20, 19:27)
- frightening (Dan. 10:7 – 'great terror', Matt. 28:3-4, Luke 1:13)

- holy (Matt. 25:31, Mark 8:38) – angels never sin!
- immortal and do not marry (Matt. 22:30, Luke 20:35-36)
- individuals (e.g. Gabriel, Dan. 8:16, Luke 1:19, Michael, Rev. 12:7)
- chosen ('elect angels', 1 Tim. 5:21)

THE WORK OF ANGELS

The work of angels includes the following:
- serving God (Ps. 103:20, Heb. 1:7, 14, Mark 1:13, Luke 22:43)
- worshipping God and Christ (Neh. 9:6, Rev. 5:11-14, Heb. 1:6)
- advertising God's character (the seraphim in God's presence constantly speak of God's holiness in Isa. 6:3; the four living creatures in Rev. 4 seem to correspond to the character of Christ in the four gospels: the kingly lion, the humble hardworking ox, the intelligent man, and the heavenly eagle, the glorious Son of God)
- messengers announcing God's purposes (the meaning of 'angels' in both Heb. *malak*, and Gk. *angelos* is 'messenger' and can refer to either human messengers, like those from Jacob (Gen. 32:3, 6), John the Baptist in Luke 7:24 and Jesus in Luke 9:52, or angels, e.g. Dan 9:21-23, Matt. 1:20, Luke 1:30, Rev. 1:1, 22:16)
- being watchers (Dan 4:13, 17, 23, Zech. 1:8-11, Luke 15:10)
- bringing judgment (an angel killed 70,000 people in 2 Sam. 24:16, struck down King Herod in Acts 12:23, and in Rev. 9:15, four angels are released to kill one third of mankind; see also Rev. 8 and 16)
- protecting God's people (Ps. 34:7, 91:11, 1 Kings 19:5, Dan. 6:22)

THE ANGEL OF THE LORD

Nearly half (90) of all OT references to angels involve the angel of the Lord. He claimed to be God (Ex. 3:2, 6), is interchangeable with God (Gen. 22:11-18, 48:15-16, cf. Ex. 13:21 and 14:19), takes God's name (Ex. 3:14, Judg.13:17-18, cf. Isa. 9:6), and receives worship (Josh. 5:15, Judg. 13:19-20). This appears to be a theophany ('appearance of God'), yet the angel of the Lord also speaks with the Lord (Zech. 1:12-13). This suggests that the angel of the Lord is actually a pre-incarnate appearance of Christ.

20 GOD'S ENEMIES: SATAN AND DEMONS

C. S. Lewis wrote: 'There are two equal and opposite errors into which our race can fall about the devils. One is to disbelieve in their existence. The other is to believe, and to feel an excessive and unhealthy interest in them. They themselves are equally pleased by both errors and hail a materialist or a magician with the same delight'[24].

Satan is the prince of rebel angels. He is powerful, 'the god of this age' (2 Cor. 4:4), who holds the whole world under his sway (1 John 5:19). He has many names:
- Satan (Matt. 4:10, meaning 'adversary')
- The Devil (Matt. 4:1, meaning 'the accuser')
- the Evil One (Matt. 6:13)
- Beelzebub (Matt. 12:24, the 'lord/ruler of demons')
- Belial (2 Cor. 6:15, referring to someone vile or wicked)
- Lucifer (Isa. 14:2, lit. 'day star')

Is Satan Real or Symbolic?
Some cults hold that Satan is not a real being, but merely a metaphor for evil. However, Satan accused Job before God (Job 1:9), desired to have Peter (Luke 22:31), and disputed with Michael over Moses' body (Jude 1:9). Christ said He saw Satan fall as lightning from heaven (Luke 10:18), and also called Satan 'the father of lies' and 'a murderer from the beginning' (John 8:44, see also 1 John 3:8-10). Only a real being can do these things. The idea of Satan is mocked in our society, and he is pictured as dressed in a red suit, with horns, a tail and a pitchfork. But Satan is found at the beginning and end of the Bible, unchanged, highly intelligent, totally evil and incredibly powerful.

> *Won't somebody step to the front forthwith, and make his bow and show,*
> *How the frauds and crimes of a single day spring up? We want to know.*
> *The Devil was fairly voted out, and of course the Devil's gone.*
> *But simple people would like to know who carries his business on.*
>
> (A. J. Hough)

Satan's Fall

Satan was 'the anointed cherub ... perfect in your ways from the day you were created till iniquity was found in you' (Ezek. 28:14); he wanted 'to be like the Most High' (Isa. 14:14). His sin was pride (1 Tim. 3:6).

Satan's Work

Satan is a deceiver (Rev. 12:9), 'the father of lies' (John 8:44), he blinds the minds of those who do not believe (2 Cor. 4:4), tempts people (Matt. 4:13, 1 Thess. 5), causes doubt (Eph. 6:16), takes people captive to do his will (2 Tim. 2:26), goes about as a roaring lion seeking whom he may devour (1 Pet. 5:8), and hinders Christians in their service (1 Thess. 2:18)

Demons are angels who rebelled against God along with the Devil (Matt. 25:41, Jude 6, Rev. 12:4 and 9). Other common names are 'unclean spirits' and 'evil spirits'. They are associated with idolatry; they desire worship, and to turn men away from the worship of the True and Living God (1 Cor. 10:20, Deut. 32:16-17). They are also involved in deceiving people in other ways, through false doctrines (1 Tim. 4:1) and ideas (1 John 4:1).

Just like angels, there are different ranks of demons (e.g. the Prince of Persia and the Prince of Greece, Dan. 10:20). Demons can also indwell and control individuals (Mark 5:1-6), causing sickness, mental disorders, physical strength (Mark 5:2-4), and self-harm (Matt. 17:15). They are cast out by Christ and others (Matt. 8:16, Acts 16:18).

The End of Demons: many demons presently exist in a prison called 'the abyss', or 'bottomless pit' (the demons in Legion pleaded not to be sent there, Luke 8:31), or 'Tartarus' (2 Pet. 2:4), where they are held in chains of darkness awaiting judgment (Jude 6), from which some or all will be released during the tribulation period (Rev. 9:1-3), and presumably sent there again during the millennium with Satan (Rev. 20:1-3). At the final judgment, Satan and his angels will be cast into the Lake of Fire forever (Matt. 25:41, Rev. 20:10).

SECTION THREE:

The Doctrine of Christ

21 THE DEITY OF CHRIST

'If He is only man, then I am an idolater. If He is very God, then the man who denies it is a blasphemer. There can be no union among those who hold His Deity and those who deny it' (G. Campbell Morgan). 'A Saviour not quite God is a bridge broken at the farthest end' (H. Moule).

OBJECTIONS TO THE DEITY OF CHRIST

We have already listed many verses directly attesting the Deity of Christ (see Ch. 18, The Trinity). Here we will look at some objections.

A. **'The Mighty God'** (Isa. 9:6). Some argue this should be translated 'a mighty warrior', and that it does not call Christ God. But in Isa. 10:20-21, the exact same words describe Yahweh as 'the mighty God'.

B. **'The Word was God'** (John 1:1). Some deny the Deity of Christ by translating this as 'the Word was *a god*'. They argue that Satan is called 'the god of this age' (2 Cor. 4:4) and that Christ is a god in the same way as Satan. However, the fact that the Word is here described as (a) existing in the beginning, (b) with (lit. 'face to face' with) God, (c) a person – He (v2), (d) the creator of all things, v3, (e) in whom was life, all seem to describe a person alongside and equal to God Himself. Satan is called a god in the sense of a false-god, not an inferior-rank god. Christ is clearly not a false-god, and to say that He is a lesser god is to deny monotheism and introduce a Greek-style pantheon.

C. **'My Father is greater than I'** (John 14:28) is pointed to as proof that Christ was inferior to God. However Christ, 'being in the form of God' (Phil. 2:6), willingly humbled Himself to become a man, and took a lowly place of subjection and obedience to His Father (Phil. 2:7-8).

D. **'My Lord and My God'** (John 20:28). Some argue that Thomas was so surprised when he saw the risen Christ that he swore. However, if so, Thomas should have been reprimanded by Christ, and if He was not God, Christ should have disowned the idea that He was 'Lord and God'. Instead, Christ congratulated Thomas for believing (John 20:29).

E. **'To the Son He says, Your throne, O God'** (Heb. 1:8). Some try to translate this as 'God is Your Throne'. Besides being virtually nonsensical, this translation makes Christ superior to God, inasmuch as a

King is more important than the seat he sits upon. The context (in both Psalm 45:6 and Hebrews 1:8) shows that these words are addressed, not to God, but to an earthly King on His wedding-day, who is therefore both God, and as the next verse shows, man ('God, Your God, has anointed You with the oil of gladness more than Your companions').

INDIRECT EVIDENCE THAT CHRIST IS GOD

Many things in the life of Christ subtly hint that Jesus is God:

1. **His Miracles**: Jesus' miracles are amazing, in their number, variety, power and effect. But Jesus does not attribute His miracles to God's power, like the OT prophets did, or NT apostles (see Acts 3:12). Instead, Jesus claimed the miracles as his own (Mark 1:40-41, 5:41, John 2:19). God 'alone does great wonders' (Ps. 136:4), yet Jesus performed the greatest miracles, doing things that God alone does (e.g. Jesus walks on the sea, John 6:19, cf. Job 9:8).

2. **His Words and Teachings**: Jesus' teachings were extraordinary, but Jesus did *not* say, 'Thus says the LORD' like OT prophets, but instead, 'Truly, truly, *I say to you*'.

3. **His Claims to Greatness**: Jesus claimed to be 'greater than the temple' (Matt. 12:6), the Sabbath (12:8), Satan (12:26-29), Jonah (12:41), Solomon (12:42), Jacob (John 4:10-12), and Abraham (8:53-58). In John 8:23 He says, 'You are from beneath, I am from above', and in John 8:42, He says 'I proceeded forth and came from God'. More startling claims could hardly be made.

4. **His claims to be Sinless**: John 8:29, 46, 55. Jesus alone, like God, is without sin.

5. **His claim to be truly Good.** He could say, 'No one is good but One, that is God' (Luke 18:19), yet also say 'I am the Good Shepherd' (John 10:11). He 'went about doing good' (Acts 10:38). Christ proved his perfect goodness by giving up all for others (2 Cor. 8:9, cf. Luke 18:22).

6. **His claims to Pre-existence**: See John 6:38, 8:58, 17:5.

7. **His claims to have a Unique Relationship with God**: God is 'My Father' (Matt. 7:21). See also John 5:18 where He describes God as 'His own Father, making Himself equal with God'.

22 THE HUMANITY OF CHRIST

'That man should be made in God's image is a wonder, but that God should be made in man's image is a greater wonder, that the Ancient of Days would be born, that He who thunders in the heavens should cry in a cradle' (Thomas Watson). 'Infinite and yet an infant, eternal and yet born of a woman, almighty and yet nursing at a woman's breast, supporting a universe and yet needing to be carried in a mother's arms, heir of all things and yet the carpenter's despised son' (C. H. Spurgeon).

1. **He had a real body.** Christ partook of 'flesh and blood' (Heb. 2:14). He had ten fingers and toes, hair that needed to be cut, and shared in all the daily routines for hygiene and cleanliness. 'The Word became flesh' (John 1:14). The hymn writer wrote, 'Oh who am I, that for my sake, my Lord should take frail flesh and die?'
2. **He had a human name.** Our Lord took a common, humble, everyday, human name. There are five different people referred to in the NT with the name Jesus (e.g. Col. 4:11), Joshua in OT.
3. **He was a real baby.** He who 'upholds all things by His powerful word' (Heb. 1:3) was Himself held in the arms of His mother as a baby. He who 'fills all things' (Eph. 4:10) was 'wrapped in swaddling cloths' (Luke 2:7), that pinned His arms and protected His naked body against cold and harm. As a toddler, He had to learn to walk and talk. 'The child grew and became strong in spirit, filled with wisdom, and the grace of God was upon him' (Luke 2:40).
4. **He was obedient to His human parents** (Luke 2:51). The Lord of all obeyed His human parents. The One who knew all things 'learned obedience by the things which He suffered' (Heb. 5:8).
5. **He was weary and hungry.** Christ was weary from a journey (John 4:6), slept on a pillow in the back of the boat (Mark 4:38) and was hungry during his temptation in the wilderness (Matthew 4:2).
6. **He had real human emotions.** He wept (John 11:35), rejoiced (Luke 10:21), was sorrowful (Matt. 26:37), compassionate (Matt. 9:36), astonished (Luke 7:9) and angry (Mark 3:5).
7. **He prayed** (Mark 1:35, Luke 6:12), trusting in God (Matt. 27:43).

8. **He was poor**. His parents offered turtledoves or pigeons at His birth – the sacrifice of the poor (Luke 2:24). He said that 'the foxes have holes and the birds of the air have nests, but the Son of Man has nowhere to lay His head' (Matt. 8:20). He did not have the money to pay the temple tax (Matt. 17:27). All He had at His death were His clothes. He was buried in a borrowed tomb. See 2 Cor. 8:9.

9. **He worked** quietly till the age of thirty as a carpenter, doing repetitive and humble jobs day after day.

10. **He was the 'Man of Sorrows'** (Isaiah 53:3). He was persecuted for righteousness' sake, for being different, for God's sake (Psa. 69:7), for not living with the same worldly ambitions as others. His brothers did not believe in Him (John 7:5), and His relatives said He was mad (Mark 3:21). He came from a disreputable village ('can anything good come out of Nazareth?' John 1:46). Israel's long-awaited Messiah was rejected by His own people (John 1:10-11).

11. **His humility**. After thirty years of perfectly pleasing God in obscurity, he was baptized in the Jordan. He did not proclaim His own sinlessness, or disclose His true identity, let alone confess any sins like all the other people, but in being baptized, He identified with all the other people. When He came up out of the water, God could keep silence no longer; but rent the heavens and proclaimed, 'This is my beloved son in whom I am well pleased' (Matt. 3:17).

12. **He tasted death**. Jesus on the cross was able to feel what was being done to him. Some Christians almost seem to think that Jesus could have stayed upon the cross indefinitely, as if He was some sort of superman or a rubberman upon whom crucifixion had no effect. But Christ was a real man. Hebrews 2:9 tells us that He 'tasted death for everyone'. He experienced death in all its terrible reality.

> *Like man He walked, like God He talked*
> *His words were oracles, His works were miracles*
> *Of man, the finest specimen, of God, the true expression*
> *Full-orbed humanity, crowned with deity*
> *No taint of iniquity, no trace of infirmity*
> *Behold the man, behold thy God* (Anonymous)

23 THE VIRGIN BIRTH

TV talk-show host Larry King was asked which person from history he would like to interview. He said Jesus Christ. "What would you have asked him?" King replied, "I would ask him if he was indeed virgin-born, because the answer to that question would define history"[25].

The Virgin Birth means that Christ was born of the virgin Mary without the involvement of a human father (Matt. 1:18-25, Luke 1:26-35). Christ's conception was supernatural, but His birth was perfectly normal. Biblical evidence for the virgin birth includes:
1. Mary said 'I do not know a man', i.e. 'I am a virgin' (Luke 1:34).
2. Joseph, 'a just man', had no part in the conception of the child and 'was minded to divorce her secretly' (Matt. 1:19).
3. Christ was conceived by the Holy Spirit (Matt. 1:18, Luke 1:35).
4. Mary and Joseph both protested their innocence, showing they knew the facts of nature. The virgin birth was not a primitive superstition.

There are a number of important reasons for the virgin birth:
- For Christ to be the God-man, the Mediator between God and men.
- For Christ to be holy and human, both sinless and a sacrifice.
- For Christ to be the Messiah, descended from David's line and a perfect King (unlike all other kings, who were sinful and failures).

Regarding the need for a sinless Saviour, it is sometimes argued that Christ was sinless because He did not inherit sinfulness through the male blood-line. However, Christ was sinless, not so much because of a lack of a human father, but because of His conception by the Holy Spirit, whose sinless nature over-rode any possibility of sin (Luke 1:35). The Roman Catholic Church teaches the doctrine of the Immaculate Conception (first officially proclaimed in 1854), by which they mean that Mary was born without sin so that Christ, too, could be sinless. However, the Bible never mentions this doctrine, nor is it true (see Job 14:4). Although Mary is highly honoured in the Bible, yet she was not virgin-born, but had normal, human parents, so she too was a sinful human being needing 'God my Saviour' (Luke 1:47). She was shown grace: 'favoured' (Luke

1:26,28) means 'be-graced'.

OBJECTIONS TO THE VIRGIN BIRTH

1. It is only mentioned in Matthew's and Luke's Gospels. This complaint might carry some weight if Christ's birth were found in only one gospel, but two accounts independently attest the same truth. In addition, we have other hints in the NT, like 'born of a woman' (Gal. 4:4), and 'the Word became flesh' (John 1:14), and the prophecy of Gen. 3:15 about the seed of the woman. If God Himself were to live on earth, we would expect something like a virgin birth.
2. Some argue that Immanuel was not to be born of a 'virgin' (Isa. 7:14), for the Hebrew word *almah* does not mean a virgin, but a 'young woman'. If so, the young woman who gives birth is already married, and the birth is not miraculous at all. However, the Jewish translators of the Greek Septuagint (c. 200 BC) used the same Greek word for virgin, *parthenos*, here as in Matt. 1:23. In none of the six other references to '*almah*' in the OT is the meaning 'a young *married* woman' apparent. In any case, how would the birth of a son to a young married woman be a 'sign' or miracle as Isaiah prophesies?
3. Many commentators insist that Isaiah's prophecy of Immanuel, 'God with us', born of a virgin (Isa. 7:14), was Isaiah's own child (although Isaiah already had children, so his wife was not a virgin, Isa. 7:3), or King Ahab's child (but Hezekiah was already born by this stage, cf. 2 Kings 16:2, 18:2), or maybe an unknown child born soon after the prophecy – otherwise, how could it have any relevance to Isaiah's time? However, Isa. 9:6 also famously foretells (a) the birth of a child, (b) who would bear the most exalted names and titles, and (c) would in fact be God. Can there really be any doubt that it is the same child whose birth is prophesied in two passages barely a page apart in our Bibles? Isa. 9:6 shows that the child does not belong to the family of a prophet like Isaiah, but rather the royal family – He will sit upon the throne of David. Isa. 7:15-16 also say that this child would be sinless: 'he shall know to refuse the evil and choose the good'. Matthew was not manipulating OT Scripture or taking texts out of their context, but reading Isaiah 7:14 in its original setting, by letting Isaiah 9:6 explain what the earlier prophecy in 7:14 meant.

24 CHRIST'S SINLESSNESS

Numerous verses in the NT attest to Christ's sinlessness.

- Peter the man of action says 'he did no sin' (1 Peter 2:22).
- Paul the man of intellect says 'he knew no sin' (2 Cor. 5:21).
- John who knew him well could say, 'In him is no sin' (1 John 3:5).
- God said 'You are My beloved Son, in whom I am well pleased' (Mark 1:11). While all the other people coming to John's baptism confessed their sins, Christ did not. After thirty years of watching Christ's perfect life, God could keep silent no longer, and rather than allow Christ to be thought a sinner like other people being baptized, He declared Christ's sinlessness from heaven.
- Hebrews 7:26 says, 'For such a High Priest was fitting for us, who is holy, harmless, undefiled, separate from sinners, and has become higher than the heavens'. Christ was not 'separate from sinners' in the sense that He avoided contact with sinners, but rather morally distinct, in being without sin.

Other verses speak of Christ being *like* us – rather than being identical with us – the difference being that He was without sin:

- Heb. 4:15: 'For we do not have a High Priest who cannot sympathize with our weaknesses, but was in all points tempted as we are, yet without sin'.
- Phil. 2:7 says, He 'made Himself of no reputation, taking the form of a bondservant, and coming in the likeness of men'. Notice it doesn't say, 'coming as a man'. There are points of likeness, but also of difference.
- Rom. 8:3 explains: 'God sending His own Son in the likeness of sinful flesh'. Here is the point of difference: Christ did not have a sinful nature like we do, because He was God.

Therefore, Christ as a man was like, or similar, to us, but not identical, for He was sinless.

COULD CHRIST HAVE SINNED?

All Christians agree that Christ did not sin, but some say that He could have sinned. They argue that Christ must have been able to sin because otherwise it would not be possible for Him to have been truly tempted, as the Bible says He was. For Jesus' temptation to have been real, He must have been able to sin.

However, this logic is false. Someone might try to tempt me to put sugar in my tea by continually telling me how wonderful tea tastes with sugar, but just because they continually talk about tea with sugar does not make me in any way *want* to drink tea with sugar, for I gave up sugar in my tea years ago and now dislike the taste. While they are tempting me outwardly, there is nothing inwardly in me that responds to their temptation. Christ's temptation, of course, was of a far severer nature. The effort Christ had to make to overcome temptation was extreme; 'with vehement cries and tears' (Heb. 5:7). We see His agony at the horror of the cross that lay before Him in the garden of Gethsemane.

The term we use to describe the fact that Christ was unable to sin is **impeccable**. The Lord Jesus spoke about this in John 14:30 when He said, 'The ruler of this world (i.e. Satan) is coming, and he has nothing in me'. We might paraphrase this verse to say, 'Satan had nothing in Christ to sink his claws into, nor was there anything he could get any grip on'.

Christ's temptation was real – his felt the pains of hunger, for example, and the dread of the cross. But the fact that this temptation was real does not mean that it was possible for him to sin. Rather, 'the resistance of temptation may be torture to a good man ... only the man who does not yield to a temptation ... knows the full extent of that temptation' (Morris[26]). In fact, we could argue that Christ's temptation in the wilderness and in Gethsemane proves to us that Christ could not sin, for if Adam sinned and fell in a garden paradise and angels disobeyed and sinned in heavenly paradise, then the fact that Christ did not sin after six weeks in the desert without food under Satanic attack or in the face of the terrible suffering of the cross, shows that he did not sin under the most extreme temptation possible. We may therefore conclude that He was unable to sin. This also shows that He was more than a mere human being or an angel – he was God.

25 THE MYSTERY OF CHRIST'S PERSON

'He was the God-man. Not God indwelling man. Of such there have been many. Not a man deified. Of such there have been none save in the myths of pagan systems of thought; but God and man, combining in one Personality the two natures, a perpetual enigma and mystery, baffling the possibility of explanation' (G. Campbell Morgan)

THE MYSTERY OF CHRIST: GOD AND MAN

How can someone be God and man at the same time? For example, Christ was weary and sat down beside a well (John 4:6), yet God is never weary (Isa. 40:28). Christ was asleep in the boat (Mark 4:38), but God never slumbers nor sleeps (Psalm 121:4). God does not hunger, He is self-existent and self-sufficient; but Christ was hungry (Matt. 4:2). No one has seen God (John 1:18), yet Christ was 'heard, seen ... and handled' (1 John 1:1). God is omnipresent (Psalm 139:7-12), but Christ was not physically present everywhere at once when on earth, although He is today by His Spirit (Matt. 18:20, 28:20). God does not change, (Mal. 3:6), yet Christ changed as he grew from a baby to a man. God cannot die – He is immortal (1 Tim. 1:17, 6:16), yet Christ died.

ATTEMPTS TO EXPLAIN THE MYSTERY OF CHRIST'S PERSON

In the past, some like the Arians denied Christ's deity, claiming He was the first created being, while Ebionites claimed God adopted the man Jesus as His Son at His baptism, and others denied His real humanity, teaching that Christ only seemed to be a man (Docetism). Others attempted to explain the mystery in various ways:

1. **Christ was part God and part man (Apollinarianism)**: Christ had a human body, but He had no human soul or spirit or mind. Instead, His soul and spirit were from His divine nature. He was 'God in a body'. 'If so, His humanity was defective and was that of an animal or an idiot' (Hoste[27]). But this is wrong: Christ had human reactions, e.g. 'troubled in spirit' (John 13:21). Christ was not half man and half God – he was fully human and divine.

2. **Christ has two separate natures (Nestorianism)**: Christ had two distinct and separate natures, one divine and one human, in the same body. In other words, Christ was not one person, but two inside the same body. But Christ did not have a split personality. He always spoke as "I", not "we".
3. **Christ had one Divine-human nature (Monophysitism)**: Christ's divine and human natures were joined together to form one new nature. On this view, Christ had a hybrid divine-human nature. The problem with this idea is that a hybrid is a third type of nature, neither truly divine nor truly human. However, Christ was truly God and truly man, not a third category.
4. **The Council of Chalcedon** in A.D. 451 convened to discuss the person of Christ, and formulated a creed which asserted that Christ had two natures (a divine nature and a human nature) in one person. It rejected the above views, stating that Christ is not a hybrid, nor two separate persons, nor defective in either deity or humanity. The mystery of how Christ can be both man and God is left unexplained. Chalcedon has been the standard of orthodoxy ever since.
5. **The Kenosis Theory**: Christ emptied Himself of some or all of His divine attributes in becoming a man. The word *kenosis* comes from Philippians 2:7 where we read that Christ 'made Himself of no reputation', or literally, 'emptied Himself' (Greek, *keno*). However, this theory denies Christ's deity: 'all the fullness of the Godhead dwelt in Him bodily' (Colossians 2:9)
6. **Milder Forms of the Kenosis Theory.** Others teach that although Christ was fully God, He lived on earth simply as a man, or like an OT prophet, dependent on God. His miracles were done in the Spirit's power, not His own (Matt. 12:28), and He was ignorant of facts (e.g. Mark 5:30, 11:13). In this scheme, Christ's deity made very little practical difference to His life or ministry. However, the NT teaches that Christ demonstrated the attributes of deity while on earth, forgiving sins, knowing the hearts of men, and rising from the dead (John 2:19, 10:18). All forms of 'kenosis theory' that argue that Christ ceased to be, or ceased to act as, God have a problem.

26 CHRIST'S DEATH

Thus far did I come laden with my sin,
naught could ease the grief that I was in
till I came hither. What a place is this!
Must here be the beginning of my bliss?
Must here the burden fall from off my back?
Must here the strings that bound it to me, crack?
Blessed cross! Blessed sepulchre! Yea, blessed rather be
the Man that there was put to shame for me.
            (John Bunyan, *Pilgrim's Progress*)

THE GOSPEL RECORDS

The accounts of Christ's death in the gospels emphasize certain important facts:

1. **Innocence**. Christ was righteous and innocent of any crime. Three people in Matthew's gospel attest this fact (Judas, 27:4, Pilate's wife, 27:19, and Pilate, 27:24). In Mark's gospel, Pilate asks 'Why, what evil has he done?' (15:14). Luke tells us that Pilate three times attested Christ's faultlessness (23:4, 14, 22), while the thief on the cross said, 'this man has done nothing wrong' (23:41). John tells us that Pilate twice attests that Christ is without fault (19:4, 6).
2. **Substitution**. The story of Barabbas is mentioned in all four gospels; Christ was taken and put to death while Barabbas, a murderer, was set free (see Acts 3:14-15).
3. **Suffering**. The gospels do not attempt to describe the physical suffering of the cross, other than to describe the drugged drink offered to Him to dull the pain, but they occupy some space detailing the emotional pain and abuse Christ suffered (a) from the soldiers, (b) from the passers-by, (c) from the chief priests, scribes and elders, (d) and even from the robbers crucified with Him. Christ was not only forsaken by his disciples and friends, but also by God (Matt. 27:46, Mark 15:34). Christ thus suffered physically, emotionally, and He was spiritually forsaken.

These three facets of the cross point to the cross as a Penal Substitutionary Sacrifice; penal in that Christ suffered, substitutionary because He died in someone else's place, and sacrificial in that Christ died, the innocent in the place of the guilty. Christ died at Passover as the sacrificial lamb.

WHO WAS RESPONSIBLE FOR CHRIST'S DEATH?

Lots of people were responsible for putting Christ to death: Roman soldiers were immediately responsible for putting Christ to death, Pilate was responsible for Christ's death (by giving the order), the Jewish rulers and council were responsible for Christ's death, the Jewish mob was responsible, for they cried for Christ's blood, and Judas was responsible.

Men were thus responsible for putting Christ to death. Peter said in Acts 3:15, '(you) killed the Prince of life'; in Acts 5:30, 'whom you murdered by hanging on a tree' (see also Acts 10:39). Satan was also responsible, in that he entered Judas to betray Christ, leading to His death.

However, in John 10:17-18 Jesus said: 'Therefore My Father loves Me, because I lay down My life that I may take it again. No one takes it from Me, but I lay it down of Myself. I have power to lay it down, and I have power to take it again. This command I have received from My Father'. Both sides of the story are true: while other people were responsible for putting Him to death (see Christ's own words in Mark 10:33-34), it is also true that Christ laid down His life of Himself. Ultimately, it was God's purpose that Christ should die for our sins; the plan of our salvation originated in God's great heart of love. Christ was the lamb slain from the foundation of the world (Rev. 13:8). Acts 2:23 says, 'Him being delivered by the determined purpose and foreknowledge of God, you have taken by lawless hands, have crucified, and put to death'.

There is also a sense in which we were responsible for Christ's death.

> *Was it for crimes that I had done*
> *He groaned upon the tree?*
> *Amazing pity! grace unknown!*
> *And love beyond degree!* (Isaac Watts)

27 THE ATONEMENT

Atonement means 'making pardon for sin'. Leon Morris has written, 'The atonement is the crucial doctrine of the faith. Unless we are right here, it matters little, or so it seems to me, what we are like elsewhere'.

THE THREE MAIN THEORIES OF THE ATONEMENT
1. **Satan-ward**: Christ's death was a ransom paid to Satan, who was unable to prevent Christ's resurrection and was thus tricked, and left with nothing. This view of Christ's death prevailed in the first millennium.
2. **God-ward**: Christ's death was a sacrifice offered to satisfy God's righteous demands against man's sin ('Penal Substitution'). Liberal theologians reject this idea, using labels like 'Cosmic Child Abuse'[28] and arguing that we should not put the emphasis upon Christ's death but rather upon his resurrection, and how we can have new life.
3. **Man-ward**: Christ's work was intended to draw man to God, as a perfect example of self-denial and non-retaliation, which we are called to follow. This contains an element of truth, but makes no sense unless Christ's death actually dealt with sin. A pilot jumping out of a plane, telling passengers that he was only doing this because he loved them, or to set them an example of non-violence or self-denial, would make no sense unless by so doing he somehow saved his passengers.

SEVEN BIBLICAL PICTURES OF WHAT CHRIST'S DEATH ACHIEVED
1. **Propitiation (Sacrificial): God's Wrath against Sin was Satisfied** (Rom. 3:25, Heb. 2:17, 1 John 2:2, 4:10). God's attitude toward our sins is wrath or anger (see John 3:36, Rom. 1:18, Isa. 64:5) and, as the Law teaches, can only be satisfied by sacrifice. Thus, the language of sacrifice is used to describe Christ's death (Eph. 5:2, 1 Cor. 5:7, Heb. 9:26, 10:12, etc). Christ's death was where God's love and wrath meet: God's wrath was revealed (punishing sin in Christ) as well as God's love (pardoning sinners).
2. **Redemption (Commercial): Christ paid the Price to Set us Free**. Here, sin is depicted as a debt that we owe to God, which has been freely forgiven because of the price paid by Christ. Eph. 1:7 says, 'In

Him we have redemption through His blood, the forgiveness of sins, according to the riches of His grace'. We have been set free from our sins, i.e. we have been forgiven. See Mark 10:45, Rom. 3:24, 1 Cor. 1:30, Gal. 3:13, 1 Tim. 2:5-6, Heb. 9:12, 1 Pet. 1:18.

3. **Justification (Legal): We have been Pronounced Righteous** (see Rom. 3:23-24, 5:9, Tit. 3: 7). God is righteous, and must condemn guilty sinners who have broken His laws, but God can justify us because 'He made Him who knew no sin to be sin for us, that we might become the righteousness of God in Him' (2 Cor. 5:21).

4. **Reconciliation (Social): We have Peace with God.** We who are separated from God by our sins (Isa. 59:1) have been restored to friendship (see Col. 1:21-22) by Christ's blood (v20), that is, by His death (v22). See also Rom. 5:10-11, 2 Cor. 5:18-20.

5. **Purification (Moral): We have Been Cleansed from Defilement.** The Bible pictures sin as dirt and defilement. To God, sin is repulsive (see Hab. 1:13, Isa. 64:6). Sin brings shame, and our conscience is stained, but Christ has washed us from our sins in His own blood (Rev. 1:5) and 'by Himself made purification for sins' (Heb. 1:3, 9:14). The one who was without spot, altogether lovely, morally perfect and unblemished, was disfigured and made an appalling sight, put to shame and publicly exposed to all (Isa. 52:14).

6. **Healing (Medical): We have been made Whole by Christ's Suffering.** Isa. 53:5 says, 'He was wounded for our transgressions, He was bruised for our iniquities; the chastisement for our peace was upon Him, and by His stripes we are healed' (see also 1 Pet. 2:24). We are healed from sin because Christ on the cross took upon Himself our transgressions, iniquities and sins. Here again, healing is a word-picture; it is not that Christ became sick for us on the cross, or that Christ's death wins physical healing. Christ was wounded, fatally (lit. 'pierced'), and he was bruised (lit. 'crushed'). He took the chastisement, the punishment, the stripes, the blows. In exchange, our wounds are healed.

7. **Victory (Military): Christ Triumphed over Powers of Darkness.** See Col. 2:14-15, Heb. 2:14-15, 1 John 3:8. Here we have a military picture. Christ defeated Satan, sin and death at the cross.

28 REASONS TO BELIEVE IN THE RESURRECTION

'After more than 700 hours of studying this subject and thoroughly investigating its foundation, I have come to the conclusion that the resurrection of Jesus Christ is one of the most wicked, vicious, heartless hoaxes ever foisted upon the minds of men, or it is the most fantastic fact of history' (Josh McDowell). 'Taking all the evidence together, there is no single historic incident better or more variously supported than the resurrection of Christ' (B. F. Westcott).

REASONS TO BELIEVE IN CHRIST'S RESURRECTION

1. Eyewitnesses

Historical events – from car crashes to murders – are verified by eyewitness testimony (Deut. 19:15). Historians do not perform scientific experiments to prove past events, e.g. that Captain Cook sailed to Australia. Instead, they rely on witnesses. The apostles witnessed the risen Christ (Acts 2:32). Paul lists eyewitnesses in 1 Cor. 15:3-8.

2. Evidence

Just as modern courts also admit other evidence, like skid marks in car crashes, the NT also presents confirming evidence: the guard, the seal, the missing body, the undisturbed grave clothes.

3. Emotions

The gospels do not set out a legal case or a logical proof for the resurrection, but tell us of the reactions of the disciples. Mary weeps (John 20:11), while the two on the road to Emmaus are confused (Luke 24:13-27). After Jesus appears to the disciples, we read of their mixed emotions: unbelieving and yet joyful at the same time (Luke 24:41). When people recount an incident, they normally describe how they felt, because our inner lives (thoughts and emotions) are the most real things in our existence. The disciples display some extremely raw emotional responses: dismissing the women's report of the empty tomb as 'idle tales' or 'silly nonsense' (Luke 24:11, lofty male scorn). Thomas resorts to crudity: putting his hand inside the body wound. The raw emotions are evidence that the reporting of the resurrection is true to real life.

THE DOCTRINE OF CHRIST

4. Effects
All historical events have continuing consequences. The fact that most people in Australia have white skin and speak English is a result of Captain Cook's visit. In the case of the resurrection, the fact that there exists a Christian church 2000 years later is consistent with the fact of the resurrection; in fact, nothing else really explains its explosive growth. Many of the early disciples were put to death for their preaching of the resurrection of Christ. Still today, transformed lives are an ongoing effect of the resurrection of Christ.

ALTERNATIVE THEORIES
1. **Swoon Theory**: Christ did not die on the cross, but merely swooned, or was drugged, and later revived in the tomb. Evidence Christ really died is seen in the blood and water of the spear wound, the centurion's confirmation of death, Christ's burial, the unlikelihood of a half-alive man rolling away the stone, or of a half-dead Christ convincing the disciples he had conquered death.
2. **Stolen Body**: Someone stole the body, either the disciples or the Jews. Evidence against this theory includes the guard set to prevent it, the story of the soldiers sleeping, which does not add up, the bribe paid to the soldiers, the undisturbed grave clothes (why not take them too?), the unlikelihood of the disciples dying for a lie, and the failure of the Jews or Romans to produce the body.
3. **Hallucination**: The disciples imagined that they saw the risen Lord. However, the empty tomb and missing body are undisputed; the disciples claimed to have touched, talked, walked and ate with the risen Christ. They did not expect Him to appear and some did not recognise Him when He did. Multiple people cannot have the same hallucination (e.g. 500 people at once, 1 Cor. 15:6).
4. **Legend**: The disciples made the whole thing up years later. However, the disciples preached the resurrection within weeks, allowing opportunity for alternative evidence to be presented. The origin and growth of the church is best explained by the resurrection; there are references in early letters to the resurrection (e.g. 1 Cor. 15:3-4). Why would the disciples be prepared to die for a lie?

29 THE RESURRECTION

'The Resurrection is the best-attested fact of history' (Matthew Arnold).

WHAT WAS CHRIST'S RESURRECTION?

1. **Not a myth, but a real historical event.** It was not a case of Christ living on in the hearts of those who loved him; it was not 'the rise of faith' among the early disciples (Rudolf Bultmann). Christ's resurrection was what caused the disciples' faith; it was not a case of their faith causing (i.e. inventing) the resurrection, for their faith had collapsed. The resurrection was an historical event.
2. **Not a case of spiritual 'life after death', it was a bodily resurrection.** Some cults teach that Christ did not rise bodily, but only 'spiritually' lived on. This is similar to popular ideas of ghosts. But the Bible teaches that Christ was physically touched by His disciples, and ate with them, in resurrection. His body was real.
3. **Not just the same physical body restored to life, it was a 'spiritual body'.** Christ's resurrection body was not simply the same body raised to life again, like Lazarus or other people, but who afterwards died again. It was the same body that had died (witness the nail-prints), however this body had undergone a transformation into a 'spiritual body' (1 Cor. 15:44), just like believers' bodies will experience a transformation at Christ's coming (1 Cor. 15:51, Phil. 3:21, 1 Pet. 3:18, lit. 'made alive in the spirit', 1 Tim. 3:16, 'justified in the spirit'). Christ's resurrection body was physical, but it was also spiritual and imperishable.

THE SIGNIFICANCE OF THE RESURRECTION

1. **It proved that He was the Son of God** (Rom. 1:4, Matt. 12:38-40, John 2:18-19).
2. **It is the basis for our faith** (Rom. 10:9). If Christ did not rise from the dead, 'we are of all men the most pitiable' (1 Cor. 15:19); our 'faith would be empty ... forgiveness would be a delusion ... future life would be a false hope' (W. Wilcox[29]).

3. **It vindicated His innocence and sinlessness.** He was 'justified in the spirit' (1 Tim. 3:16). Because He was God's Holy One His resurrection was a moral necessity (Acts 2:24, Psalms 15, 16).
4. **It demonstrated God's satisfaction in the finished work of His Son.** He was 'raised from the dead by the glory (or, approval) of the Father' (Rom. 6:4). If Christ had committed even one sin, He could not have been raised; the resurrection proves His work was perfect.
5. **It provided the means for our justification.** Rom. 4:25 says, 'he was delivered up because of our offences, and was raised because of our justification'. The resurrection is faith's object (Rom. 10:9).
6. **It proved that death is overcome and conquered.** Christ has returned again from the abyss, the bottomless pit (Rom. 10:7). 'I am He who lives, and was dead, and behold, I am alive forevermore. Amen. And I have the keys of Death and Hell' (Rev. 1:18).
7. **It was a victory over Satan** (see Heb. 2:14-15).
8. **It means that believers should live a new life**, in which we die to sin, our old man is crucified with Christ, and we walk in newness of life (Rom 6:1-11), not living any more for ourselves but for Christ (2 Cor. 5:15, Gal. 2:20), we seek the things which are above (Col. 3:1).
9. **It provides the basis for baptism by immersion** (Rom. 6:3-4, Col. 2:12); baptism pictures death, burial and new life.
10. **It means that we serve a living Saviour.** He is with us (Matt. 28:20, Heb. 13:5), He shepherds us (Heb. 13:20) and intercedes for us (Romans 8:34).
11. **Christ's resurrection is the guarantee of our future resurrection** (see 1 Cor. 15:20-23). He is 'the first to rise from the dead' (Acts 26:23), 'the firstborn from the dead' (Rev. 1:5).
12. **Christ's resurrection gives assurance of a judgement to come** (see Acts 10:42, 17:30-31).

'The evidence for Jesus' resurrection is so strong that nobody would question it except for two things: first, it is a very unusual event, and second, if you believe it happened, you have to change the way you live' (Wolfhart Pannenberg[30]).

Section Four:

The Doctrine of The Holy Spirit

30 THE PERSON OF THE HOLY SPIRIT

'The two great outstanding facts of the present time ... are (1) that a Man sits at the right hand of God in heaven, and (2) that the Third Person of the Godhead is a Resident upon this planet' (H. P. Barker).

THE DEITY OF THE HOLY SPIRIT

The Holy Spirit is God (the 'Spirit of God', 26 refs., the 'Spirit of the LORD', 28 refs). He is called God in Acts 5:3-4; in 1 Cor. 3:16, because of the Spirit's indwelling, we are a 'temple of God'.

The Holy Spirit Shares God's Unique Characteristics: He is **Eternal** (Heb. 9:14), **Omnipresent** (Ps. 139:7), **Omniscient** (1 Cor. 2:10-11), **Omnipotent** (having God's power: Isa. 11:2, Luke 4:14, 11:28, Matt. 12:28), **Life-creating** (Rom. 8:2, Psalm 104:30, Job 33:4), **Spiritual Life-Creating** (John 3:6-7, Titus 3:5, cf. John 1:12-13, 1 John 5:1), **Raises the Dead** (Romans 1:4, 8:11, cf. John 5:21, 28), **Inspires Scripture** (1 Tim. 3:16, 2 Peter 1:21), **Holy**, the 'Holy Spirit' (96 refs. in the Bible, cf. Lev. 19:2, Josh. 24:19, 1 Sam. 2:2, Job 6:10, Isa. 1:4, 6:3 and Luke 1:35). **The unforgivable sin** of 'blasphemy against the Holy Spirit' (Matt. 12:31) suggests that the Holy Spirit is Divine.

The Holy Spirit, the Father and the Son are One: The Holy Spirit is called both the 'Spirit of God' and the 'Spirit of Christ' (Rom. 8:9), 'the Spirit of His Son' (Gal. 4:6), 'the Spirit of Jesus Christ' (Phil. 1:19, see also 1 Pet. 1:11 and Acts 16:7 'the Spirit of Jesus'). Christ dwells in us (Rom. 8:10, 2 Cor. 13:5, Col. 1:27, Eph. 3:16-18), so the Son and the Spirit are One (cf. John 14:16-18, and Rev. 2:7).

THE PERSONALITY OF THE HOLY SPIRIT

The Holy Spirit is a Person, not a 'force', influence, or the 'power of God at work in the world'. The Holy Spirit is described as 'He' (see John 14:26, 15:26, 16:13-14) and 'who' (not 'which' Eph. 1:13-14). He speaks of Himself as "I" (Acts 10:20, 13:2). He is the 'Helper' (John 14:16, 26, 15:26, 16:7), 'Comforter' (KJV) or 'Counsellor' (NIV), which means 'someone called alongside' to help, guide, encourage, or be an advocate (1 John 2:1). This word describes a Person, not a force or influence. He is called 'another' Helper (John 14:16), and so like Christ Himself, and therefore a Person. The Holy Spirit has personal qualities: He can be grieved (Isaiah 63:10, Eph. 4:30), jealous (James 4:5), He has a will (1 Cor. 12:11), can speak (Acts 8:29, 1 Tim. 4:1), hear (John 16:13), pray and intercede (Romans 8:26), He comforts (Acts 9:31), convicts (John 16:8), encourages (John 14:16), can be sinned against (Matthew 12:31), lied to (Acts 5:3-4), He witnesses, testifies (John 15:26), leads, guides (John 16:13), teaches (John 14:26) and forbids (Acts 16:6, 7).

THE DISTINCTIVENESS OF THE HOLY SPIRIT, FATHER AND SON

The Holy Spirit is placed alongside the Father and the Son in the Bible: Isa. 48:16, Matt. 28:19-20, 1 Cor. 12:4-6, 2 Cor. 13:14, Eph. 3:16-19, 4:4-6, 2 Thess. 2:13-14, Heb. 2:3-4, 9:14, 1 Peter 1:2 and Jude 20-21. He is equally God and yet distinct (see John 14:16 and Christ's baptism).

THE CHARACTER OF THE HOLY SPIRIT

He is **Gentle** – He is the Comforter, the Dove, **Humble** – not glorifying Himself but Christ (John 16:14), **Patient** – not forcing Himself upon people, **Sensitive** – grieved by sin, jealous, quenched, **Holy** – separate from any sin, and **Loving** – He is the Helper, He gives us gifts. As God, He is great and mighty, yet He humbly saves, serves and sanctifies us. What an incredible Person!

PICTURES OF THE HOLY SPIRIT IN SCRIPTURE

Wind (John 3:8, Acts 2:2), Oil (1 Sam. 16:13, Luke 4:18, Acts 10:38, 2 Cor. 1:21, 1 John 2:20), Water (John 3:5, 7:38-39), Dove (Matt. 3:16), Fire (Acts 2:3), Tongues (Acts 2:3), Seal (2 Cor. 1:22, Eph. 1:13, 4:30).

'If He is merely a power or influence, our dominant aim would be, how may I obtain more of His power and influence? But if He is a Divine Person, our consistent attitude should be, how can He more fully possess me so that I may become the vehicle of His power and influence?' (J. Oswald Sanders, *The Holy Spirit and His Gifts*).

31 THE WORK OF THE HOLY SPIRIT

THE WORK OF THE HOLY SPIRIT IN THE OLD TESTAMENT

There are about 90 references to the Holy Spirit in the Old Testament (and about 250 in the NT). In the OT, the Holy Spirit:

1. **Created and gave life**: (Gen. 1:2, Psalm 33:6, Job 26:13, 33:4, Ps. 104:30). God spoke the world into existence, by His 'breath', as the Hebrew word Spirit, *'ruach'* is often translated.
2. **Spoke through people**, i.e. as people prophesied (Num. 11:25-29, 24:2, 1 Sam. 10:6, etc.).
3. **Inspired Scripture.** (1 Pet. 1:11).
4. **Convicted of sin.** (Gen. 6:3, Neh. 9:30, Zech. 7:12).
5. **Taught and Instructed** God's people (Neh. 9:20, Ps. 143:10).
6. **Led people.** (Psalm 143:10, Isa. 63:14).
7. **Indwelt** Joseph (Gen. 41:38), Joshua (Num. 27:18), Ezekiel (Ezek. 2:2), Daniel (Dan. 4:8). He 'clothed' Gideon (Judg. 6:34).
8. **Filled people**: Bezaleel building of the Tabernacle (Ex. 28:3, 31:3) and Joshua (Deut. 34:9).
9. **Gifted people**: Tabernacle workmen (Ex. 28:3, 31:3), Joshua (Deut. 34:9, with wisdom), certain judges with leadership (Judg. 3:10), Daniel (Dan. 5:12)
10. **Empowered people.** Samson (Judg. 13:25, 14:6, 19, 15:14), but see also Micah 3:8.

THE WORK OF THE HOLY SPIRIT IN THE NEW TESTAMENT

In the NT, the Holy Spirit performs all of the same ministries that He performed in the OT: He is the **'Spirit of life'** (Romans 8:2) who 'gives life' (2 Cor. 3:6, see also Matt. 1:18, John 3:5, Rom. 8:11), He **speaks** through people (i.e. prophesies, 1 Corinthians 12:7,10, see also Acts 2:17, 19:6), He **inspires Scripture** (2 Tim. 3:16), He **convicts** the world of sin, righteousness and judgment (John 16:8), He **teaches** God's people (John 14:26), He **leads** disciples (Rom. 8:14, Gal. 5:18), He **indwells** believers (John 14:17, Rom. 8:9), He **fills** people (Luke 1:15, Acts 2:4), He **gifts** God's people (1 Cor. 12:4), He **empowers** saints (Acts 1:8).

The Distinctive Work of the Holy Spirit in the NT

Christ said that the Holy Spirit had not yet been given (John 7:39). Christ also spoke about His coming in the future tense (John 16:7-8, 14:26, 15:26). Some argue that the difference is that the Holy Spirit only came *upon* people in the OT, but in the NT, He *indwells* believers (John 14:17). But, the Holy Spirit indwelt Joseph (Gen. 41:38), Joshua (Num. 27:18), Ezekiel (2:2) and Daniel (4:8). The following are some of the distinctive features of the work of the Holy Spirit in the NT:

1. **The Holy Spirit comes upon Believers Universally.** In the OT, the Holy Spirit only indwelt certain leaders, for certain tasks. In the NT He is given to all believers (Acts 2:17-18, Heb. 8:7-12).
2. **The Holy Spirit comes Permanently upon Believers in the NT.** In the OT, the Holy Spirit left certain people like Saul (1 Sam. 16:14), and Samson (Judg. 16:20). But in the NT, John 14:16 says, 'I will give you another Helper that He may abide with you forever'.
3. **The Holy Spirit comes upon people in New Birth.** In the OT, someone became a member of the people of God by being born into the Jewish race. But in the NT, entry into the church is by being born again of the Spirit (John 3:3-8, Tit. 3:5, 2 Pet. 1:4).
4. **Decentralised Religion**: In the OT, God was specially present in one place: the Temple. In the NT, God's Spirit indwells all believers – we are his temple (1 Cor. 6:19). See John 4:21.
5. **Inward Religion**: In the OT, religion involved ceremonies, but people's hearts were far from God (Isa. 1:10-17, Amos 4:1-5; 5:21-24). In the NT, we worship in 'spirit and in truth' (John 4:23-24).
6. **Unity and Diversity**: Because of the coming of the Spirit, the church is characterised by unity. All who have the Spirit are one in Christ. Yet, there is also diversity – and not just racially, socially, or economically. We have different gifts of the Holy Spirit (Rom. 12:3-8, 1 Cor. 12:1-26).
7. **Freedom**: The Holy Spirit brings Freedom, cf. the OT and its law (Gal. 5:18). 2 Cor. 3:17 says, 'Where the Spirit of the Lord is, there is freedom'. The Holy Spirit should be free to work through His servants, using their gifts. The Church is not an institution, but a living, indwelt organism.

32 THE HOLY SPIRIT AND THE BELIEVER

The Pentecostal movement, which started in the United States in 1901, taught that all Christians should seek a post-conversion experience called the Baptism with the Holy Spirit, evidenced by speaking in tongues. The Charismatic renewal movement dates to the 1960s and saw the spread of speaking in tongues to other denominations, including the Roman Catholic Church. The 1980s saw the arrival of the 'Third Wave', emphasizing the use of signs and wonders in the preaching of the gospel. The Prosperity Gospel developed out of Pentecostal and Charismatic roots, teaching that not only healing but wealth are to be claimed by faith. The Toronto Blessing of 1994 saw animal noises and 'holy laughter' (also called being 'drunk on the Holy Spirit'), as well as people shaking and jerking, being claimed as manifestations of the Holy Spirit. What shall we make of the modern Pentecostal/Charismatic emphasis upon the Holy Spirit? Has the Holy Spirit been sent to help us speak in tongues, make animal noises, laugh hysterically or to help us become healthy and wealthy? Here we shall look at what the NT says about the work of the Holy Spirit in the life of the believer.

THE ROLE OF THE HOLY SPIRIT IN THE BELIEVER'S LIFE: ROM. 8
Romans 8 has 18 references to the Holy Spirit, more than any other NT chapter. Here are seven things the Holy Spirit does in the believer's life:

1. The Spirit sets us Free from Sin (Rom. 8:2)
Romans 7 teaches that we are captives of 'the law of sin' (7:23). But Romans 8:2 says that 'the law of the Spirit of life in Christ Jesus has set me free'. How does the Holy Spirit set us free from sin? Not by the law – which stirs up sinful desires (Rom. 7). Rom. 8:5-7 says the Spirit frees us as we set our mind on the things of the Spirit. As we set our minds on Christ, our minds are renewed (Rom. 12:2, Col 3:2), we are transformed and become more like Christ (2 Cor. 3:18).

2. The Spirit Indwells Us (v9)
Every true Christian is indwelt by the Holy Spirit. Rom. 8:9 says that 'if anyone does not have the Spirit of Christ, he is not His'. We cannot have one-third of the Trinity. It is all or nothing. See also John 14:17.

3. The Spirit Sanctifies us (v12-13)

Verses 12-13 tell us that we are not to live for the flesh, but for God. We do so by mortifying (putting to death) the deeds of the body. Rom. 8:13 says that sanctification is an ongoing process, not a once-for-all event: 'if you by the Spirit are putting to death the deeds of the body'. Nor is it a passive process: we actively put to death the deeds of the body. Holiness is an ongoing, lifelong work of the Holy Spirit in us.

4. The Spirit leads us (v14)

Rom. 8:14 teaches that the Holy Spirit leads us as Christians (see also Gal. 5:18). While the Holy Spirit leads us in life's decisions, the Spirit's work is primarily to lead us in this process of becoming more holy.

5. The Spirit bears witness (v15-17)

The Holy Spirit within us causes us to cry out, Abba Father, and in so doing He bears witness with our spirit that we are children of God. He gives us assurance that we truly belong to God as we cry out to Him as Father (see also Gal. 4:6, 1 Cor. 12:1-3).

6. The Spirit fills us with hope (vs18-25)

We have 'the firstfruits of the Spirit' (v23), a foretaste of the future transformation of the entire Creation (v21) when our Lord Jesus reigns.

7. The Spirit helps us by interceding for us (v26-27)

The Holy Spirit helps us in our weakness and sinfulness.

Conclusion: the Holy Spirit's main work in our lives is that we might be conformed to the image of God's Son (Rom. 8:28-29).

Other roles of the Spirit: He Sanctifies (2 Thess. 2:13, 1 Pet. 1:2) – that is, sets us apart for special dealings leading to salvation, Convicts of sin (John 16:18), Regenerates (i.e. brings about the 'new birth', John 3:5, 8, Titus 3:5, 1 Peter 1:22), Seals us (2 Cor. 1:22, Eph. 1:13), Anoints us (1 John 2:20, 2 Cor. 1:21-22), Guarantees our salvation (2 Cor. 1:22, 5:5, Eph. 1:23), Fills us (Acts 2:4, Eph. 5:18), Teaches us (John 14:17, 26; 16:13-15, 1 Cor. 2:9-16), Gives Gifts (1 Cor. 12:4, Heb. 2:4), Strengthens us (Eph. 3:16), Reveals God to us (Eph. 1:17-19), Helps us to pray (Eph. 2:18; 6:18, Jude 20), Comforts us (Acts 9:31), Empowers us (Acts 1:8, Eph. 3:16), Speaks through us (Acts 2:17-18, 1 Cor. 12:1-2), Unifies God's people (Eph. 2:18, 22; 4:3, 1 Cor. 12:13), and Guides us (Acts 8:29, 10:19-20; 13:2; 16:6, 7).

33 THE BAPTISM IN THE HOLY SPIRIT

There are three main views about the baptism in the Holy Spirit (not the 'baptism *of* the Holy Spirit'):
1. It was something that happened once-for-all at Pentecost, not an individual experience so much as a corporate event, by which all believers were mystically formed into one body, the Church.
2. It happens to every believer at conversion. It is simply another term describing what happens when a person receives Christ and becomes a member of His universal church.
3. It is a post-conversion event that all believers should experience, 'the Second Blessing', with power to witness and authority to live a victorious, holy life, evidenced by speaking in tongues.

THE BIBLICAL EVIDENCE

There are seven NT references: Matt. 3:11, Mark 1:8, Luke 3:16, John 1:33, Acts 1:5, 11:16 and 1 Cor. 12:13. In **the Gospels**, John the Baptist foretells the coming of the One who 'will baptize you with the Holy Spirit and fire' (Matt. 3:11). The fire here refers, not to Pentecost, but to Hell, for the fire in verses 10 and 12 is where the unsaved are sent, cf. Luke 3:17. The baptism in the Holy Spirit and in fire are opposites; baptism in the Holy Spirit is the opposite of going to Hell and is equivalent to being saved. John was not foretelling the blessing of speaking in tongues, or the corporate unity of the church, or power for service, but the blessing of salvation through Christ.

In **Acts 1:4-8**, the baptism in the Spirit results in power for service, as is still true today (see Eph. 3:16). But, while power is one of the results of the baptism in the Spirit; it is not what the baptism in the Spirit fundamentally involves or means. In **Acts 11:15-17 (and 15:8-9)**, Peter points out that the Holy Spirit falling upon the Gentile believers was the same thing that happened to the Jewish believers (Acts 11:15-17). This would mean that here we have two separate instances of people being baptized in the Holy Spirit – not one, never-to-be-repeated event. 'God ... acknowledged them by giving them the Holy Spirit ... *purifying* (or, cleansing) their hearts by faith' (Acts 15:8-9). The Holy Spirit came upon the Gentile believers as proof that they were forgiven by God. Again, therefore, the baptism in the Spirit refers to the cleansing from our sins at conversion (see also Tit. 3:5).

In **1 Cor. 12:13**, all Christians have been 'baptized into one body and have all been made to drink one Spirit'. This verse stresses the consequence of the baptism in the Spirit: there is one body. However, again, Christian unity, or becoming part of the one body, is a result of Spirit baptism, not its essence. We became part of the united body of Christ at conversion (not at Pentecost). This passage disproves the idea that the baptism in the Spirit is an empowering for service, as evidenced by speaking in tongues, for 'all' believers have been baptized in the Holy Spirit. But in this chapter, all have different gifts (12:4, 11, 29, 30) – not all are apostles, or prophets, nor do all speak in tongues. This means that we may be baptized in the Holy Spirit but not speak in tongues.

What about the Evidence of Post-Conversion Experiences in Acts?
Various people spoke in tongues in Acts on receiving the Spirit: the first disciples (Acts 2), the Samaritans (Acts 8), Cornelius (Acts 10) and the Ephesian disciples (Acts 19). However, all of these cases either involved unique situations (Pentecost), or were a visible demonstration of the unity of Spirit (Samaritans and Gentiles), or occurred at conversion (Acts 19). The New Testament never tells any believers to pray for, or seek for, the baptism in the Holy Spirit, their 'personal Pentecost'.

Theological and Practical Problems with the 'Second Blessing'
We cannot have part of the Trinity at salvation (Christ, but not the Holy Spirit), see Rom. 8:9-11. If we do not have the Holy Spirit, we are not Christians at all. Eph. 1:13 tells us: 'believing, you were sealed with the Holy Spirit of promise'. All Christians are fully blessed in Christ (Eph. 1:3, Col. 2:9); there are not two classes of Christians (those with and without the Second Blessing). Those arguing that speaking in tongues is an evidence of the indwelling Holy Spirit call into question the salvation of people who are unable to speak in tongues.

Summary: the baptism in the Spirit is what happens at conversion: 'the washing of regeneration and renewal of the Holy Spirit' (Tit. 3:5).

34 THE FILLING OF THE SPIRIT

'I believe the Bible teaches there is one baptism in the Spirit – when we come to faith in Christ ... [but] many fillings – in fact, we are to be continuously filled by the Holy Spirit ... It is not how much of the Spirit *we* have, but how much the Spirit has of *us*' (Billy Graham[31]).

In the Bible there are fourteen individuals or groups of people said to be filled with the Spirit:
- In the OT: Bezaleel (Exod. 31:3 and 35:31), other Tabernacle craftsmen (Exod. 28:3), and Joshua (Numbers 34:9). Also possibly Micah 3:8 and Num 14:24.
- In the Gospels: John the Baptist (from birth, Luke 1:15), his mother Elizabeth (Luke 1:41), his father Zacharias (Luke 1:67), and Jesus (Luke 4:1).
- In the book of Acts: the disciples on the day of Pentecost (Acts 2:4), Peter (Acts 4:8), all the believers gathered to pray (in Acts 4:31), Stephen (Acts 6:5, 7:55), Paul (Acts 9:17, 13:9), Barnabus (Acts 11:24), and all the disciples in Antioch (Acts 13:52).

The following qualities are associated with these people who were filled with the Spirit: praise (Elizabeth, Zechariah, Simeon, Luke 1 and 2), boldness (the apostles and early Christians, Acts 4:8, 13, 31), faith (Stephen, Acts 6:5; Barnabus, Acts 11:24), power (Stephen, Acts 6:8, Paul, Acts 13:9-11), wisdom (the seven, Acts 6:3, see also Exodus 31:3, Deut. 34:9), understanding and knowledge (Exodus 31:3, 35:31), revelation (Stephen, Acts 7:55), joy (the disciples in Antioch, Acts 13:52), prophecy (Zechariah and Elizabeth, Luke 1:41, 1:67), speaking in tongues (the disciples on the day of Pentecost, Acts 2:4).

WHAT DOES IT MEAN TO BE FILLED WITH THE SPIRIT?
Ephesians 5:18-21: 'Do not be drunk with wine, in which is dissipation (a loss of self-control), but be filled with the Spirit'. We notice:
1. The verb is in the imperative mood – it is a command. All Christians should be filled with the Spirit.

2. The verb is in the present continuous tense: 'keep on being filled with the Spirit'. It is an ongoing need in the believer's life, rather than a once-for-all, never to be repeated event (like baptism in the Spirit). Why do we need to be continually filled with the Spirit? D. L. Moody: 'because we leak'.
3. The verb is in the passive voice: It is not something we do, but something that happens to us.
4. Being filled with the Spirit is the opposite of being drunk; a person is not out of control, but instead fully controlled by God's Spirit, and perfectly in control of himself and his faculties.
5. Being filled with the Spirit is associated with wisdom, understanding God's will, singing, thankfulness and submission (vs 17-21).

Other qualities commonly associated with the Holy Spirit include love (Eph. 3:16-19), peace (Rom. 14:17, 15:13), righteousness (Rom. 14:17) and hope (Rom. 15:13, Gal. 5:5). Paul's prayer in Eph. 3:16-19 shows that to be filled with the Spirit is to be filled with Christ Himself.

How are we filled with the Spirit?
Some verses seem to tell us how we may be filled with God's Spirit.
1. We should pray that we might be filled (Luke 11:13, Acts 4:24-31, Eph. 3:16ff., Rom. 15:13).
2. In Col. 3:16-17, the parallel passage to Eph. 5:18-21, Paul, instead of speaking about being filled with the Spirit says, 'Let the word of Christ dwell in you richly in all wisdom'. We are filled with the Spirit as we fill our minds with God's Word. We should come like Mary to sit at His feet – for the Spirit's work is to point us (not to himself), but to Christ.
3. We should surrender our lives to Christ, by 'presenting ourselves to God' (Rom. 6:13, 12:1-2), so that we die to self and live to Christ.
4. We should not grieve the Spirit by sin (Eph. 4:30). The Spirit is jealous when we follow the world (James 4:5). We need to confess our sins to enjoy fellowship with God (1 John 1:9).
5. We need to be continually 'being filled' (Eph. 5:18), to 'die daily' (1 Cor. 15:31, 2 Cor. 4:16).

35 THE GIFTS OF THE SPIRIT

There are four main passages in the New Testament dealing with spiritual gifts: Rom. 12:6-8, 1 Cor. 12-14, Eph. 4:7-16 and 1 Pet. 4:10-11. These passages teach three general lessons.

1. All believers have spiritual gifts. 'As each one has received a gift, minister it to one another as good stewards of the manifold grace of God' (1 Pet. 4:10); 'but to each one of us grace was given according to the measure of Christ's gift' (Eph. 4:7); 'the manifestation of the Spirit is given to each one for the profit of all' (1 Cor. 12:7).
2. There is a great variety of spiritual gifts. Rom. 12 mentions seven gifts, 1 Cor. 12:8-11 mentions nine (and the other gift-list at the end of chapter 12 mentions another four, and in chapters 12-14 there are about twenty different spiritual gifts mentioned), Eph. 4:11 mentions five, and 1 Pet. 4:10-11 mentions the two broad categories of speaking and serving.
3. The NT urges individual Christians to use their gifts. 1 Pet. 4:10 says, 'as each one has received a gift, minister it to one another'. Rom. 12:6-8 says, 'Having then gifts differing according to the grace that is given to us, *let us use them*: if prophecy, in proportion to our faith ...'. We are responsible for using our God-given gifts.

HAVE SOME SPIRITUAL GIFTS CEASED?

Some argue that because 'Jesus Christ is the same yesterday, today and forever' (Heb. 13:8), then all the gifts of the early church are still in operation today. However, God is not still inspiring books of Scripture today, and most Christians agree that there are no apostles today; they were foundational (Eph. 2:20). Some argue that 1 Cor. 13:8 teaches that miraculous gifts (like prophecy, tongues and healing) ceased with the completion of the canon of Scripture. It is argued that 'when that which is perfect (or 'complete') is come' (v10), i.e. the canon of Scripture, 'then that which is in part will be done away', referring to these 'sign gifts'. However, the context is against this argument. The 'when' of verse 10 refers to 'then' of verse 12, so that when the 'perfect' comes then we will see 'face to face' and 'know just as I also am known'. Seeing Christ 'face to face' and having perfect knowledge will only happen in heaven. If the completed canon of Scripture were in view here, the passage would be saying that, with the entire Bible, we now know just like God knows us, with a face to face knowledge of Him. This not only exaggerates the state of our present knowledge, but also means that we know more than the apostle Paul who said that he only knows 'in part' (v9).

There is no verse that says that some gifts ceased with the completion of the canon of Scripture. Yet Hebrews 2:4 says, 'God also bearing witness both with signs and wonders, with various miracles, and gifts of the Holy Spirit, according to His own will'. This verse teaches that the purpose of gifts was as a witness and sign, and it also teaches that God sovereignly distributed these gifts 'according to His will' (see also 1 Cor. 12:11), so that God may give (or withhold) such gifts as and when He pleases. God does not promise constant miracles; in fact, there were four main periods of miraculous activity in the Bible: at the Exodus, at the time of Elijah, during the ministry of Christ and in the book of Acts. We are not promised constant miracles in every age. On the other hand, we should not limit what is possible with God. In a yet-future day, miracles and prophets occur during the tribulation period (see Rev. 11).

Evidence that 'speaking in tongues' does not truly occur today:
- there is nothing supernatural about modern speaking in tongues – even atheists can produce it. Pagan cultures (e.g. voodoo cults, African tribes, Tibetan monks) around the world do so too[32].
- Non-Christian cults (Mormons) and teachings (Mary worship) also claim validation from speaking in tongues, and liberal theologians are confirmed in their unbelief of Scripture via speaking in tongues.
- scientific studies of speaking in tongues have found no evidence of known human languages, or of real language. It consists of repetitive combinations of syllables with simulated foreign accents[33].
- As someone has said, "If you claim to speak in the language of angels (1 Cor. 13:1), you prove it".

This evidence renders the claim that modern 'speaking in tongues' is a manifestation of the Holy Spirit untenable.

SECTION FIVE:

The Doctrine of Man

36 THE DOCTRINE OF MAN

'What a piece of work is a man! How noble in reason, how infinite in faculty, in form and moving how express and admirable, in action how like an angel, in apprehension how like a god' (Shakespeare, *Hamlet*).

WHAT IS MAN?

Man is more than a body. We have a non-material part to our existence, given to us by God. Verses which speak of our God-given 'spirit' include Num. 16:22, Heb. 12:9, 23. Our body is just a tent we live in for a while (2 Cor. 5:1-4, 2 Pet. 1:13, 14), a vessel in which we are carried around (1 Thess. 4:4). In 2 Cor. 12:2, Paul was caught up to Paradise, unsure whether he was in the body or out of it. The entire message of the Bible depends upon the idea that man has a spirit, for if we deny the existence of spirits, we deny the existence of God, who is a spirit (John 4:24), angels, who are 'ministering spirits' (Heb. 1:14), the Devil and demons, the possibility of the Holy Spirit indwelling us (1 Cor. 6:19), and the Bible's teaching that, after death, our souls and spirits live on.

Atheists argue that man is nothing more than matter, a carbon-computer, a machine made of meat, a highly intelligent animal. However, there are good evidences that we are more than just chemical reactions. We possess (1) rationality – the ability to think, understand, create, and invent, (2) free will – the ability to make deliberate choices, (3) morality – the knowledge of right and wrong, (4) consciousness – our 'inner life', a first-person awareness of ourselves, (5) qualia – the ability to experience beauty, and (6) personality – we experience life as an individual, a unity.

SOUL AND SPIRIT

Trichotomists argue that we have three parts: body, soul and spirit (1 Thess. 5:23), and that the soul and spirit are different (Heb. 4:12). Both the OT and NT have a different word for soul and spirit. On the other hand, 'soul' and 'spirit' are hard to distinguish as Heb. 4:12 says. **Dichotomists** argue that there are only two parts to man (the physical and the immaterial), and that the terms 'spirit' and 'soul' are interchangeable. Verses supporting this view include Luke 1:46-47, the fact that at death we read of the 'soul' departing and at other times, the 'spirit' departing but not both (Soul: Gen. 35:18, 1 Kings 17:21, Luke 12:20; Spirit: Ecc. 12:7, John 19:30, Acts 7:59).

Wrong Ideas: (1) the spirit is the higher part of us which relates to God (but both soul and spirit can worship and pray, Ps. 103:1, John 4:23, Ps. 25:1, 1 Cor. 14:14), (2) the soul is at some sort of 'lower level' than the spirit: but the spirit is involved in knowing and thinking (Ex. 31:3, Ps. 77:6, Mark 2:8, 1 Cor. 2:11-14, cf. Ps. 139:14), feeling and emotion (Gen. 26:35, lit. 'grief of spirit', Ps. 51:17, John 13:21, Acts 17:16, 2 Tim. 1:7) and moral dispositions (Num. 5:14, Ps. 34:18, Matt. 5:3, 2 Tim. 1:7), (3) our spirit comes alive at conversion (but see James 2:26; unbelievers have a spirit: Pharaoh, Gen. 41:8, Sihon, Deut. 2:30).

The **spirit** (Heb. *ruach*, Gk. *pneuma*) seems to be the immaterial part of our being, which gives us our abilities of rationality, free will, consciousness, conscience, and, because it is immaterial, the part of us which will outlive death (eternity). The words for '**soul**' (Heb. *nephesh*, Gk., *psyche*) are commonly translated simply as 'life' (Gen. 19:17, Ex. 21:23, Mt. 2:20, Mt. 20:28, John 10:11, Acts 20:10), even of animals: Gen. 1:21, 24 ('creatures'). Sometimes 'soul' refers to the 'self' (Luke 12:19, Luke 1:46.), or the 'personality' (Luke 10:27), or 'people' (Acts 2:41, 43, 7:14, 27:37, Rom. 13:1 and 1 Pet. 3:20) or 'anyone' (Lev. 2:1). Sometimes 'soul' refers to the immaterial part of our being (Matt. 10:28, Acts 2:27, 3 John 1:2), and sometimes to its faculties of mind, will or emotion (Ecc. 6:9, 'desire', Gen. 23:8, 'wish', 'mind', Deut. 21:14, 'will', KJV, Acts 14:2, Phil. 1:27, Mark 14:34, Heb. 12:3).

It would seem that the soul is not a part of our make-up (like the spirit, or the body), but rather 'the real me', the 'self', the unique personality that is us (see Gen. 2:7). 'Man does not possess a *psyche*, as if it were a suitcase or an umbrella, but he *is* a *psyche*' (George Carey). 'You do not have a soul. You are a soul. You have a body' (C. S. Lewis). The soul does not need a body to live. It can and will live on in our spirit after our body dies. On the other hand, animals have a certain amount of 'personality' (loyal, friendly), but no spirit that lives on after death.

37 MAN'S ORIGIN

'The Holy Scriptures ... reveal that man's origin was not from below but from above; that he is not the creature of chance, but of God' (Hoste).

The Bible teaches that God made us (Ps. 100:3, 139:14, Job 10:8). In Gen. 1:27 we read 'God created man in His own image; in the image of God He created him; male and female He created them' (see also Matt. 19:4). The Bible nowhere teaches that man evolved from some other animal or hominid (man-like, sub-human) or some creature that had developed physically into man and just required a spirit, which God breathed into him. Others hold to the idea that Adam is legendary or represents 'everyman' in his fall into sin. However:

a) Scripture uses the word 'created' to describe man's origin (Genesis 1:27), rather than any word which might be taken to mean 'evolved'.
b) it says he was made from the dust of the earth (Genesis 2:7), not from a 'hominid'.
c) it calls him 'the first man' (1 Cor. 15:45, 47), indicating he was real, not legendary.
d) Eve was created from Adam's side (Gen. 2:21-22), not born from sub-human ancestors (see also 1 Cor. 11:8-9). If we accept that Adam developed from pre-human ancestors but Eve was a special creation, this would make Eve more significant than Adam.
e) Adam was not a legendary or mythical creature, for the OT speaks of him as historical, tracing his creation, marriage, sin, life-span and descendants (Gen. 5:3-4). OT Scriptures that speak of God's creation of man include Deut. 4:32 and Jer. 27:5.
f) The NT affirms Adam's creation as part of Christ's genealogy (Luke 3:38), Christ affirms Adam and Eve's creation (Matthew 19:4), Paul mentions Adam and Eve (Rom. 5:12-14, 1 Cor. 15:22, 45, Eph. 5:30-32, 1 Tim. 2:14-15) and Jude mentions him in Jude 14. The NT confirms Adam's reality as equally historical with our Lord Jesus Christ.

MADE IN THE IMAGE OF GOD

Man is special because man is made in God's image and likeness (Genesis 1:26). This does not mean that we look like God (for God is a Spirit, John 4:24). Rather, we are like God:

1. in our personality, having feelings, freedom, the ability to think, create and communicate,
2. in having a spiritual, non-material part to our constitution,
3. in that we live forever,
4. in that we are relational and social creatures, using language, just as God is a Trinity,
5. in that we are able to have fellowship with God himself, and
6. in that we have been given dominion over the earth.

That we are made in the image of God means:

a) all human life is valuable (e.g. murder is forbidden because of God's image, Gen. 9:6),
b) the image of God is universal; every person has dignity; we are made of 'one blood' (Acts 17:26),
c) we still carry the image of God even though it is distorted through the effects of sin (Jam. 3:9),
d) we carry a moral responsibility to be like God,
e) work is good, inasmuch as God worked, and we are to be like Him,
f) caring for the creation, just like God, is part of our 'dominion' responsibility,
g) Christ is the perfect 'image of God' (Col. 1:15, and we are to imitate Christ in this, Col. 3:10).

WHERE DO OUR SOUL OR SPIRIT COME FROM?

Creationism teaches that God creates a new soul for each person and sends it into the body sometime between conception and birth (Ps. 33:15, Zech. 12:1, Isa. 42:5, 57:16). However, would this not make God responsible for the sinful soul within the person? **Traducianism** teaches that the soul is inherited from the father and mother just like the body, but there is no direct Bible proof for this view. Perhaps both man and God are involved, for we inherit a sinful nature from our parents (Ps. 51:5), but we also have a spirit that is God-given and God-like.

38 MAN'S PURPOSE

'If there is no God, then man and the universe are doomed. Like prisoners condemned to death, we await our unavoidable execution. There is no God, and there is no immortality. And what is the consequence of this? It means that life itself is absurd … that the life we have is without ultimate significance, value, or purpose' (W. L. Craig).

Blaise Pascal (1623-1662) was a French mathematician and philosopher who became a Christian at age 31. He was someone who understood the despair and darkness of life without God. As Pascal describes it, man is an infinitely small speck compared to the universe and eternity. We live in a world of suffering, evil and injustice. We try to live a happy and meaningful life, but in reality, life is full of anxiety and boredom. Despite our insignificance, we are the only thinking thing in the universe. We know we are miserable, and we know the universe will one day crush us. Where is man's hope to be found? Pascal wrote: 'What else does this longing and helplessness proclaim, but that there was once in each person a true happiness, of which all that now remains is the empty print and trace? We try to fill this in vain with everything around us, seeking in things that are not there the help we cannot find in those that are there. Yet none can change things, because this infinite abyss can only be filled with something that is infinite and unchanging—in other words, God himself. God alone is our true good' (*Pensées*, 425).

It is only by God's revelation in the Bible that we learn the purpose of life. Life is not a giant mystery, nor a joke being played upon us. Solomon in Eccles. 1:2, having turned from God and His ways, looked back over his life as an old man. He had found life empty and full of frustration. He had sought intellectual fulfilment (solving great problems), fulfilment in pleasures, in laughter, in wine, fulfilment in achievements (great building projects), then in wealth and possessions. His opinion of life was 'Vanity of vanities, all is vanity', (or, 'Meaningless! All is meaningless!').

However, in the Bible we learn that the reason why God created us and put us here was that we might know Him, enjoy fellowship with Him and glorify Him. Here is another reason why man is special: he has been made for fellowship with God. God made a creature like Himself, for fellowship with Him. He didn't put us here primarily to be friends with the animals or to be gardeners. It is a great privilege for us, mere creatures, made from dust, to know the Great and Eternal God and to have fellowship with Him. People who experienced this include:

- Adam and Eve, who apparently enjoyed this before their fall.
- Enoch 'walked with God', as did Noah (Gen. 5:22, 6:9).
- Abraham was called 'the friend of God' (James 2:23).
- Moses knew God 'face to face' (Exod. 33:11, Num. 12:8, Deut. 34:10).
- In the Tabernacle, God showed his desire for fellowship: 'Let them make Me a sanctuary, that I may dwell among them' (Ex. 25:8).
- David says, 'One thing I have desired of the LORD, that will I seek: that I may dwell in the house of the LORD all the days of my life, to behold the beauty of the LORD, and to inquire in His temple' (Ps. 27:4).
- In the New Covenant, God promised that 'they shall all know me, from the least of them to the greatest of them, says the Lord, for I will forgive their iniquity and their sin I will remember no more' (Jer. 31:34).
- Paul said in Philippians 3:10 that his life's ambition was to 'know Him', that is, Christ.
- Jesus Himself said in John 17:3 that the purpose of eternal life is 'that they may know You, the only true God, and Jesus Christ whom You have sent'.

Life without God is ultimately meaningless and empty. God wants each of us to come to know Him, have fellowship with Him, and glorify Him by living a life worthy of our Maker. The Westminster Larger Catechism says, 'Man's chief and highest end is to glorify God, and fully enjoy Him forever'. Augustine wrote, 'You have made us for Yourself, O Lord, and our heart is restless until it rests in You' (*Confessions*).

39 HUMAN DESTINY

Augustine wrote, 'Life is a misery, death an uncertainty. Suppose it steals suddenly upon me, in what state shall I leave this world? When can I learn what I have here neglected to learn? Or is it true that death will cut off and put an end to all care and all feeling? This is something to be inquired into... Such great and wonderful things would never have been done for us by God, if the life of the soul were to end with the death of the body. Why then do I delay? Why do I not abandon my hopes of this world and devote myself entirely to the search for God and for the happy life?'

The Bible teaches us that when we die our spirit and soul do not die but live on. Because each one of us has a spirit from God (Heb. 12:9), it is eternal like God. Death does not end it all. Bible references for people living on after death include:

1. Jesus said to the dying thief, 'Assuredly, I say to you, today you will be with Me in Paradise' (Luke 23:43).
2. He said, 'Father, into Your hands I commit My spirit' (Luke 23:46).
3. Jesus said that 'God is not the God of the dead, but of the living' (Matt. 22:32), arguing that since God called Himself the God of Abraham, Isaac and Jacob, these men must not be dead, but continuing to live on as disembodied spirits.
4. At the transfiguration, Moses and Elijah (who had died and been translated) talked with Jesus and were still very much alive.
5. Stephen said, 'Lord Jesus, receive my spirit' (Acts 7:59).
6. Paul said, 'For to me, to live is Christ, and to die is gain'. He desired 'to depart and be with Christ, which is far better' (Phil. 1:21, 23).
7. Paul said, 'We know that if our earthly house, this tent, is destroyed, we have a building from God, a house not made with hands, eternal in the heavens' (2 Cor. 5:1). He was 'well pleased rather to be absent from the body and to be present with the Lord' (2 Cor. 5:8).
8. In Heb. 12:23, we learn that in heaven there are 'the spirits of just men made perfect'.

9. Jesus told of a man who died, was buried, and in Hades (which, in Greek, means 'unseen', i.e. the Unseen realm after death) he lifted up His eyes being in torments (Luke 16:19-31).
10. 'You will show me the path of life; in Your presence is fullness of joy; at Your right hand are pleasures forever more' (Psa. 16:11), 'As for me, I will see Your face in righteousness; I shall be satisfied when I awake in Your likeness' (Psalm 17:15), 'You will guide me with Your counsel and afterward receive me to glory' (Psa. 73:24).

The fact of human dignity also suggests that there is life after death, for such an exalted creature, created in the image of God, with all its unique and special mental and. spiritual capabilities, transcends the merely physical plane, and surely outlives earthly existence. Even most non-Christian cultures have believed in the existence of the soul after death (e.g. by placing things in the tomb with the dead person for their use in the afterlife). Even our bodies are not finished when we die. God who created our bodies is going to one day raise them back to life again (see John 5:28, 29, Revelation 20:12).

Word Pictures for Death in the Bible
- Death is the abyss, the bottomless pit (Rom. 10:7, Rev. 9:1, 11:7, 17:8, 20:1-3), 'the depths of the earth' (Psa. 71:20), 'the depths of hell' (Prov. 9:18), 'the pit ... in the lowest place of the earth' (Ezek. 26:20), the 'lowest pit, in darkness, in the depths' (Psa. 88:6). Death is like falling off the edge of a dark bottomless chasm.
- Death is like drowning under the waves of the bottomless sea (see 2 Sam. 22:5, Psa. 68:22, 42:7, 88:7, and Jonah 2:3).
- Death is like someone being cast adrift forever (Psalm 88:4).
- Death is the land of forgetfulness (Psa. 88:12), of those whom God remembers no more (Psa. 88:5, see also Psa. 31:12), like a prison where people are abandoned forever.
- Death is the place of no return, 'the place from which I shall not return, ... the land of darkness and the shadow of death' (Job 10:21, 16:22), a one-way journey into darkness.
- Death is called Hades (NT), Sheol (OT), meaning the 'unseen' realm on the other side of death.

40 MALE AND FEMALE

MEN AND WOMEN ARE EQUAL IN DIGNITY AND WORTH

Various verses in Genesis tell us about men and women being created equal in dignity: Gen. 1:27 (God's image-bearers), 2:18 ('helper') and 2:19-22 (companionship). The NT affirms these truths: men and women are 'heirs together of the grace of life' (1 Pet. 3:7), those who are saved are spiritually one in Christ Jesus (Gal. 3:22-28 – as sinners yet equally recipients of the blessing of salvation through faith in Christ), indwelt by the Holy Spirit (1 Cor. 12:13), and all have spiritual gifts (1 Cor. 12:4-7). Thus, man are woman are equal ontologically (that is, in being).

MEN AND WOMEN ARE FUNCTIONALLY DIFFERENT

Genesis 2 also teaches us that there are important differences between men and women: God created the man first (in 2:7), then the woman (2:21); the woman was derived from the man (2:21, not an independent or autonomous creature); she was created for the man, so that he would not be alone, and to be a helper for him, (Gen. 2:18). She was under the man's authority in relation to the work in the garden (2:15), in relation to the warning about eating from the tree of the knowledge of good and evil (2:16-17, this warning was given before the woman was made), and the man was given authority to name the animals (and the woman) – just as God had naming-rights in Gen. 1 as Creator, so the man is given naming rights in Gen. 2 as the person in authority in creation.

The NT repeatedly picks up on these themes, and reinforces them:
- The man is the head of the woman (1 Cor. 11:2-16, Eph. 5:23), 'head' referring to a position of authority and leadership (e.g. Num. 1:4, 25:15, Josh. 11:10, 22:14, Judg. 11:11). Biblical headship does not carry the idea of intrinsic superiority (see 1 Cor. 11:3: although Christ is equal with God the Father, Phil. 2:6-8, he voluntarily took a place of humble obedient submission).
- The NT teaches that men and women have different roles in life, with men working to provide for their families (2 Thess. 3:6-12), while women take the main responsibility for being homemakers

(Tit. 2:5) and bringing up children in the family (1 Tim. 2:15, 5:10, 14, Tit. 2:4). Wives are told to submit to their husbands (Eph. 5:22, Col. 3:18, 1 Pet. 3:1).
- Men and women have different roles in the church, the men leading and speaking publicly whereas the women are not to take positions of authority or speak publicly in the church (see 1 Cor. 14:34-35, 1 Tim. 2:11-15, 1 Tim. 3:1-13 and Titus 1:5-11).

Modern Western society has rejected the idea of complementary gender roles (as taught in the Bible), labeling male headship and female submission 'sexist'. There are many ways in which men and women are equal (e.g. intelligence), but there are also many ways in which they are designed to do different things. This is God's plan in creation:
- Men are, on average, taller and stronger than women, with 65% greater lower-body strength, 45% higher vertical leaps, and over 22% faster sprint times[34]. The only Olympic sport in which men and women compete is equestrian: the horses do all the heavy lifting.
- Men and women choose different careers. In Scandinavia, after decades promoting sexual equality, male engineers still outnumber females ten to one, while the opposite is true of nurses[35].
- The equality agenda is flawed. Everybody has different natural abilities: some are good at art, or music or athletics or mechanics. 'In this regard, all men are NOT created equal, because some are smarter, or stronger, or more talented than others' (Wiersbe[36]).

MEN AND WOMEN ARE TO BE UNITED IN MARRIAGE.

Genesis 2 shows us how God brought the man and the woman together in a complementary and harmonious partnership, marriage, to form a family, the building-block of society. This is not a master-slave relationship, but a relationship built upon companionship, love and respect. It is a relationship with different roles. If the man is to be the head of the family, the woman is the heart. Christ commended marriage (Matt. 19:4-6). The NT teaches the husband to love and the wife to respect, producing a harmonious and happy relationship (Eph. 5:22-33, Col. 3:18-19, 1 Pet. 3:1-7).

41 HUMAN NATURE

Non-Christians hold a variety of views on man's nature:

1. **Atheistic humanists** believe that humans are basically **good**. Humanists instead believe that it is only society which spoils our nature. But society is simply human nature writ large. If society is a corrupting influence, this tells us that individual humans are corrupt too. As psychologist Dr. Chris Thurman writes, 'One of our more treasured notions is that people are basically good ... I want to tell you in no uncertain terms that people are not basically good. People are basically selfish, self-centred, dishonest and deceitful'[37].

2. **'Liberal Progressives'** believe that man is **improving**. D. R. Davies (a disillusioned liberal) wrote, 'The Great War caught Liberal Christianity unawares. It broke in on it like a gangster in a drawing room full of old maids sipping their afternoon tea. It took the lid off that human nature of supposed fundamental goodness'. Communism and Nazism followed, and showed ever-deeper levels of human wickedness. The first point in Davies' statement of faith was this: 'I believe that man is radically evil, that sin is of the very texture of human nature'[38]. C. E. M. Joad was a famous 20th Century agnostic philosopher who became a Christian late in life. He had 'believed that there is no such thing as sin, that man was destined for a Utopia; that given a little time, man would have heaven on earth ... [but] Two world wars and the imminence of another had demonstrated conclusively to him that man was sinful'[39]. Progressives argue that the solution to man's problems is education, but if this were true, why was highly-educated and cultured Germany the cause of so many problems in the twentieth century?

3. **New Age Religion** holds that we are **gods**. Shirley Maclaine, the New Age actress, encourages people to 'tell yourself that you are god'. Because we are gods, Maclaine says 'it is not possible to judge another's truth' – we cannot judge anything that another person does as right or wrong, good or evil. Tolerance is the great virtue of New Age religion. Instead of judging others, we are told to 'be true to yourself' and 'follow your heart'. 'Each person must listen to the "God within" to determine his own ethical system, but he may never hold others accountable to his

system. Nothing is ever really wrong, ironically, except judging other people's moral beliefs and actions' (David Noebel[40]).

THE BIBLE TEACHES THAT MAN IS A SINNER

Gen. 6:5: 'Then the LORD God saw that the wickedness of man was great in the earth, and that every intent of the thoughts of his heart was only evil continually'. Rom. 3:23 says, 'For all have sinned and fall short of the glory of God'. See also 1 Kings 8:46, Psa. 14:1-3, 130:3, 143:2, Eccles. 7:20, and Col. 1:21. The Bible teaches that man is sinful by nature (Eph. 2:3), as well as practice. We are not sinners because we sin: we sin because we have a sinful nature. Psa. 51:5 says: 'Behold, I was brought forth in iniquity and in sin my mother conceived me' (see also Psa. 58:3, Rom. 5:19, Mark 7:21-23, Jer. 13:23, 17:9, Job 15:14-16).

EXPERIENCE TELLS US THAT WE ARE SINNERS

Man's history is written in blood and tears; every page is smeared with marks of cruelty, greed and folly. That man is sinful 'is a matter of universal experience' (Hammond[41]). 'The Christian ... "knows that it is so". He is himself a sinner. He did not at any point in his individual life choose to leave unbroken personal goodness for sin. He was sinful before he sinned' (Handley Moule[42]). Evidences of our innate sinfulness and the universal extent of sin are seen in a child's natural disobedience, tantrum-throwing, and jealousy, locks on our doors, tickets for our buses and trains, looting in cities when the police are held back, invigilators to monitor academic examinations, the fact that nearly half of all marriages nowadays end in divorce, and while half of the world is starving to death, in the West our number one killer is heart disease from overeating. 'There is none righteous, no, not one ... there is none who does good, no, not one' (Rom. 3:10).

'Most [people] believe that their major problem is something that has happened to them, and that their solution is to be found within. In other words, they believe that they have an alien problem that is to be solved with an inner solution. What the gospel says, however, is that we have an inner problem that demands an alien solution – a righteousness that is not our own' (R. Albert Mohler Jr.[43]).

Section Six:

The Doctrine of Sin

42 THE DOCTRINE OF SIN

'No thoughtful student of Scripture can fail to be arrested by the dominant place accorded in its pages to 'sin'. Its existence may indeed be considered the very raison d'être of the revelation of God to man as we have it in Holy Scripture. The word and its cognates occur upward of 2,000 times or twice on every page of the Bible. It is impossible to open the Book and not encounter it. The characters depicted (with one notable exception) are all of them sinners and every degree of wickedness is described and recorded with relentless faithfulness throughout the Book. Indeed there is no book in the world that deals so comprehensively with the subject in all its dark ugliness as does the Bible and nowhere is its condemnation so faithfully proclaimed nor the doom of sinners so plainly stated' (M. Goodman).

Definition: Sin is when we do wrong in word, deed and thought, when we know what is good, and fail to do it. Sin is when we are self-centred instead of loving God and others. All sin is primarily against God.

- **Augustine**: Sin is 'a perverse desire of height, in forsaking Him to whom the soul ought solely to cleave … when the soul abandons Him to whom it ought to cleave as its end, and becomes a kind of end in itself'.
- **Blaise Pascal**: 'This I is hateful. It is essentially unjust, in that it makes self the centre of everything; and it is troublesome to others in that it seeks to make them subservient; for each I is the enemy, and would be the tyrant, of all others'.
- **Luther**: 'man curved in on himself'.

BIBLICAL DEFINITIONS OF SIN

- Doing what is not right: All unrighteousness is sin (1 John 5:17).
- Not doing what is good: to him who knows to do good and does not do it, to him it is sin (Jam. 4:17).
- Lawlessness: Whoever commits sin also commits lawlessness, and sin is lawlessness (1 John 3:4).
- Unloving and harmful behaviour: love does no harm to a neighbour; therefore love is the fulfilment of the law (Rom. 13:10).
- Unbelief: whatever is not from faith is sin (Rom. 14:23).

- Evil Thoughts: The devising of foolishness is sin (Prov. 24:9).
- Failure to be like God: all have sinned and fall short of the glory of God (Rom. 3:23).

The Bible uses many different terms to refer to sin:

Sin (Heb. *chatah*, Gr. *hamartia*) means to miss the mark or target. It means to fail or fall short of the required standard (Rom. 3:23).

Iniquity (Heb. *avon*, from a verb meaning to 'bend or twist'): crookedness, the opposite of uprightness, any deviation from God's right ways.

Unrighteousness (Gk. *adikia*): doing what is not right (1 John 5:17).

Rebellion (Heb. *pesha*), the deliberate decision not to do God's will.

Transgression (Heb. *abar*, Gk. *parabasis*): crossing boundaries, breaking rules (Matt. 15:2-3, Rom. 4:15, 5:14; Gal. 3:19; Heb. 2:2, 9:15).

Lawlessness (Gk. *anomia*), an anti-authoritarian streak of opposition to God and His laws (1 John 3:4). The word **wicked** (Heb. *rasha*) is often translated by *anomia* in the LXX, and means 'wicked, criminal' (Brown, Driver, Briggs). It speaks of someone doing wrong wilfully.

Ungodliness. This word (Gk. *asebia*, lit. 'not worshipping') means a lack of proper respect for God our Creator. It is the 'disregard for, or defiance of God's Person' (Vine). See Rom. 1:18, 21.

Abomination, (Heb. *shiqquts*, *to'ebah*) speaks of God's revulsion at certain sins (e.g. idolatry, Deut. 7:25-26; homosexuality, Lev. 18:22; witchcraft, Deut. 18:9-12). Certain sins are more serious and heinous than others.

Guilt (Heb. *asham*, Gk, *enochos*): the consequence of sin. Guilt is not a feeling but a fact, the crime of breaking God's laws. See Jam. 2:10.

DENIALS OF SIN

Amoral non-Christians do not like the idea of sin. They think that:
- 'Ethics is just aesthetics'[44], a matter of personal likes and dislikes.
- Conscience is nothing more than social conditioning.
- Sin is an illusion (in Christian Science, like sickness).

The problem comes when people run up against raw evil. Our hearts ache over injustice and cruelty in the world. No one says it is an illusion when their car is stolen, or dismiss the sense of felt wrong as social conditioning. We excuse our own wrongs, and accuse others (Rom. 2:15).

43 SIN'S ORIGIN

The Bible describes 'the Fall' (when Adam sinned) as a real event, not an allegory. Besides the account in Genesis 3 itself, the Fall is referred to elsewhere (Job 31:33, Isa. 43:27, Hos. 6:7, Rom. 5:12-21, 1 Cor. 15:21, 2 Cor. 11:3, 1 Tim. 2:14).

Evidence from experience shows that the Fall is true:
1. the fact of sin in our world: 'Does not the condition of the world, with its daily round of wretchedness, sin and crime, agree better with the doctrine of the Fall, than with the hypothesis of evolution [i.e. with its doctrine of progress]?' Nevertheless, 'so great is man's innate pride and hostility to God that he would prefer to have risen from the apes, than fallen from God' (Hoste[45]).
2. the alien nature of sin: 'If man is not a fallen creature, why does he deplore his condition and not acquiesce in it as his natural and proper state without regret or demur?' (M. Goodman[46]).
3. the universal spread of sin: there is no branch of the human race, nor is there any individual in its history (save One), that has not been affected by sin. The fact that all men are sinners is best explained by the fact that we all belong to the same family, and share the family characteristics inherited from Adam who sinned.
4. the innate sinfulness of human beings; from the earliest age, we sin, showing that the problem is not in our nurture, but in our nature.
5. The root cause of the problem; some such event must have poisoned the human race at its start, infecting every person. It has been said that had there been no story of the fall in our Bibles we should have been compelled to invent something of the kind to account for human history.

Why did God forbid Adam to eat from the tree in the garden? The reason appears to be because Satan had already fallen, and the tree was a test as to whether man would follow in Satan's steps in rebellion or obediently follow God. Satan urged the woman to take the fruit of the tree arguing that 'you will be like God'. This had been Satan's desire also – to be like God. Adam and Eve were tempted not simply with the fruit on a physical level, but also with the opportunity to be like God (and thus be independent equals). The test showed whether the man and woman would submit to God as their Maker and Lord.

What were the results of the Fall? God had said that eating the fruit would result in certain death. Adam and Eve did not die physically, however their fellowship with God was broken and they hid from Him in the garden. The Bible speaks about man as being 'dead in trespasses and sins' (Ephesians 2:1), 'alienated from the life of God' (Ephesians 4:18) and, upon conversion, 'passing from death to life' (John 5:24). Physical death did follow eventually, as part of the curse, by which man was forced to labour hard for his bread, woman had pain in childbearing and the natural world was cursed with death. Adam's sin had ongoing effects for the rest of the human race: 'through one man sin entered the world and death through sin, and thus death spread to all men' (Rom. 5:12).

Original Sin is the term that describes the fact that we have inherited a sinful nature from Adam. Romans 5:19 says 'by one man's disobedience many were made sinners'. We don't have to wait long in the Bible to see the transmission of a sinful nature: Cain murdered his own brother.

Pelagius (ca. 350-418), a moralistic British monk, denied that humans are sinners by nature. He believed that humans can even live sinless lives, that there was no such thing as original sin (i.e. Adam's sin has not affected us), that physical death was not a result of sin, humans have a free will unaffected by sin, and that God's grace was only needed in assisting us, so we can save ourselves. Pelagianism has been described as 'justification by common decency'. Augustine (360-430 AD), converted from a life of sinful pleasures and worldly wisdom, taught that humans are sinful by their very nature, and even our 'free will' has been corrupted by sin, so that we cannot do what is good even if we desire to. Instead, salvation was entirely of God's grace. Pelagianism was condemned as heresy by various church councils from 412 to 431 A.D. However, by the middle ages, the Roman Catholic Church was Semi-Pelagian, teaching that God's grace was earned by human efforts and church sacraments. It was against this system that Luther protested in the Reformation.

44 SIN'S CONSEQUENCES

1. **Separation from God.** The purpose of our existence is fellowship with God. However, as Isaiah 59:2 says, 'Your iniquities have separated you from your God and your sins have hidden His face from you'. Adam and Eve were banished from the garden as a picture of the separation from God and all that is good. God, who is holy and pure, cannot have fellowship with a sinful and unholy world. Sin has spoiled the very purpose for which we were created. Sin has also ruined our world – not simply because men are selfish, jealous, rude, lawless and violent – but also because God cursed our world with death when Adam sinned.

2. **God's wrath or anger.** Our sins do not simply estrange us from God, they bring upon us His anger. Romans 1:18 says 'the wrath of God is revealed from heaven upon all ungodliness and unrighteousness of men'. John 3:36 says that 'he who does not believe the Son shall not see life, but the wrath of God abides upon him'. Furthermore, God promises that there is a 'day of wrath' coming (Romans 2:5). See also Romans 2:8, 9 and Psalm 50:21.

3. **Death.** Romans 1:32 tells us that 'the righteous judgement of God' is 'that those who practise such things are deserving of death'. This verse is telling us that our sins are so serious we deserve to die for each of them. The Greek word 'practice' ('commit', KJV, Gk. *prasso*, as opposed to *poieo* used later in the verse for the habitual continuance in sin), means that a person committing a single sin deserves to die. Similarly, Romans 3:25 teaches that, 'in His forbearance God had passed over the sins that were previously committed' in OT times. That is, God did not visit death upon men each and every time sin was committed, because He knew of the coming sacrifice of Christ at Calvary. If we sin we do not deserve to live in God's world any longer. We forfeit the right to live. Romans 6:23 says 'The wages of sin is death'. Because of the seriousness of sin, there is only forgiveness by sacrifice. Death is the price to be paid for sin (see Heb. 9:22). This was why the Son of God came (see Heb. 9:26).

4. **Judgment**. The Bible teaches that 'it is appointed for men to die once, but after this the judgment' (Hebrews 9:27). We might ask why there is a judgment at all: surely God knows whether we are sinners or not, and where we are going after death. The purpose of the judgment is to convict all men of the justice of their eventual sentence and to demonstrate God's righteousness and fairness. What is the basis of judgment? The Bible consistently teaches that we will be judged by our works. Thus, the three main extended treatments of the judgment in the NT teach that we will be judged according to our works (see John 5:28, 29, Romans 2:6, Rev. 20:12-13). Because we have all sinned, our works only condemn us as sinners. As Revelation 20 says, only those found written in the Lamb's book of Life through faith in Christ, saved by the blood of the Lamb, will escape Hell.
5. **Hell**. Our soul and spirit cannot die because they came from God (the Father of spirits, Hebrews 12:9); they are eternal like God Himself. This means that when we die as sinners we will be separated from God for ever. Jesus said in John 8:21 'You will die in your sin. Where I go you cannot come'. Not only will we be barred from heaven with God, but we will depart 'into the everlasting fire, prepared for the Devil and his angels' (Matt. 25:41), the Lake of Fire (Rev. 20:10-15). This is described as 'everlasting punishment' (Matt. 25:46), 'torments' (Luke 16:23) and 'wailing and gnashing of teeth' (Matt. 13:42). God's punishment of sin is inescapable (Rom. 2:3) and inveterate – it will never grow old or cold, tire or end.

BIBLICAL PICTURES OF SIN

- **Leprosy** (Lev. 13 – 14) pictures sin in its spread, separation, damage and defilement. **Leaven** (yeast) is similar (1 Cor. 5:6-8, Gal. 5:9).
- **Slavery**: see John 8:34, Rom. 6:17.
- **Darkness**: see Rom. 1:21, Eph. 4:18, Rev. 3:17.
- **Debt**: Matt. 18:23ff., Luke 7:40ff., Rom. 4:4.
- **Deceit**: Heb. 3:13, Jer. 9:17; sin promises satisfaction but fails to deliver. It is like a drug, being addictive and unfulfilling.
- **Death**. We were 'dead in trespasses and sins' (Eph. 2:1, cf. 4:17).

SECTION SEVEN:

The Doctrine of Salvation

45 THE DOCTRINE OF SALVATION

Christianity is a religion of salvation. Here are seven truths about salvation from Ephesians 2:1-10.

1. **We need to be saved** (Eph. 2:1-3). We need to be saved because of our sin (we were 'dead in trespasses and sins'), because we were dragged along in the current of the world's empty pursuits ('we walked according to the course of this world'), and we were under the power of Satan ('according to the Prince of the power of the air', see also Col. 1:13, 'the authority of darkness'). We were disobedient to God ('sons of disobedience'), 'fulfilling the desires of the flesh and the mind'. We were 'children of wrath', under God's anger. The first step to becoming a Christian is to recognise our need to be saved.
2. **Salvation comes from God** (Eph. 2:4-10). 'But God' (Eph. 2:4): God is the Saviour. Salvation is a result of the riches of **God's mercy** (His pity and compassion on us) because of **God's great love** for us (John 3:16). He loved us 'even when we were dead in trespasses and sins' (cf. Rom. 5:8). We did not have to clean ourselves up, turn over a new leaf, or try to improve our behaviour to gain God's love. Verses 5 and 7 tell us that God saved us because of the exceeding riches of His **grace** (His 'kindness or goodness', giving us something we did not deserve as a free gift). Verse 8 in fact says that salvation is God's free **gift** (see also Romans 6:23). We cannot buy salvation, earn it, or deserve it. Finally, verse 10 tells us that salvation is **God's work**: 'we are His workmanship'. Salvation is of the Lord (Jonah 2:9).
3. **Salvation is based on Christ's work.** Verse 7 speaks of being saved by the exceeding riches of God's grace in His kindness towards us **in Christ Jesus**. This refers to Christ's death for us: 'Christ died for our sins' (1 Cor. 15:3, see also Rom. 3:24, 8:32, Gal. 1:4, 1 Tim. 2:5, 6). We are not saved (A) by God letting 'bygones be bygones', (B) simply because we repent ('the confession of a criminal affords no righteous ground for his release', Hoste[47]), or (C) because of our good deeds – God requires perfect holiness, not simply more good deeds than bad. 'The Bible is unequivocal in its claim that the remission of sins and the justification of a soul before God are entirely on the basis of our Lord's atoning sacrifice' (Hammond[48]).

The Doctrine of Salvation

Hebrews 9:22 says 'without shedding of blood there is no remission (i.e. forgiveness)'. When Christ said 'It is finished' (John 19:30), it meant that there was nothing more to pay. Only Christ's death can deal with our sins.

4. **Salvation is not of works** (Ephesians 2:9). We cannot save ourselves by good works, church membership or religious observances (see also Rom. 3:20, Gal. 2:16, Titus 3:5). Another way of saying this is that salvation is not of ourselves (Eph. 2:8). Even when we try to keep God's high standards we find that we are 'without strength' (Romans 6:6) to be truly good, or to overcome our natural tendency to sin. Romans 3:12 says 'There is none who does good, no, not one'. Even the good that we do is 'like filthy rags' (Isaiah 64:6) in God's sight, corrupted by wrong motives. It is because we are so helpless to save ourselves that we need to be saved by God.

5. **Salvation is by faith**. We are saved through faith, that is, by believing in our Lord Jesus Christ (John 3:16, Acts 10:43, 16:31), receiving Him (John 1:10-12), believing the gospel (Mark 16:16, Romans 1:16). This does not mean that we believe in God (in a vague and general way), but we put our trust in Christ for salvation. Faith is not an act that earns us merit. Faith is the condition of salvation. For many people, salvation by faith seems too simple, and they want to add something to it. But salvation is by grace alone, by Christ alone, through faith alone.

6. **Salvation produces good works**. Eph. 2:8-10 says three things about works. Firstly, we are not saved by our works ('not of works, lest anyone should boast'). Secondly, we are saved by God's work ('we are His workmanship'). Thirdly, we are saved to do good works ('created in Christ Jesus for good works which God before prepared that we should walk in them'). Good works do not earn salvation, but salvation results in good works. If someone claims to be a Christian but shows no sign of turning from sin, they are probably not.

7. **Salvation is eternally secure**. Ephesians 2:5 and 8 say 'by grace you *have* been saved'. It is an accomplished fact, not something we might have, or hope to gain. It is a present possession. Eph. 2:7 tells us that 'in the ages to come, He (God) might show the exceeding riches of His grace in His kindness toward us in Christ Jesus'. We will eternally enjoy God's kindness.

46 JUSTIFICATION

In medieval times, Roman Catholic popes lived as princelings, in luxury, immorality and corruption. Pope Leo X wished to rebuild St. Peter's Basilica in Rome, and decided to raise the revenue from the poor of Europe by the sale of indulgences, offering people the forgiveness of sins upon the payment of money. Tetzel, the chief of his travelling salesmen in Germany, claimed to have saved more souls through indulgences than the apostle Peter through his preaching. He offered pardons, without any need for repentance, not only for the sins of the living, but also of the dead suffering in purgatory. He said, "Listen to your parents and your friends who are dead, and who cry to you from the depths of the abyss: 'We are enduring horrible tortures! A small alms would deliver us. You can give it, and you will not!'" Tetzel even had an advertising jingle: 'The moment the coin in the coffer rings, the soul from purgatory springs'. Martin Luther objected to the sale of indulgences by nailing 95 theses to the door of the castle church in Wittemberg on October 31st, 1517. At the heart of the Luther's protest was the doctrine of justification by faith. Luther had discovered through his study of the Bible that God justifies sinners, not on the basis of payment of money, or works, or prayers, or penances, or pilgrimages, but simply through faith in Christ.

WHAT JUSTIFICATION MEANS

Justification is a word taken from the courts of justice. It means to be pronounced 'not guilty', or to be declared righteous, by the judge. The amazing truth of justification is that God justifies, not the good person, but the ungodly (Rom. 4:5) and the sinner (Rom. 3:23-24). How is it possible for a holy and righteous God to justify the wicked? By 'His grace through the redemption that is in Christ Jesus' (Rom. 3:24), that is, the price paid by Christ's death. God pronounces guilty sinners righteous if they believe in Christ (Rom. 3:22). Justification is not found in the sacraments of the Church (baptism, confession, the Eucharist) or through works, either of self-denial, penance or charity. No religious rituals or payment of money provide forgiveness of sins. Justification is a free gift of God's kindness, based on Christ's death, received by faith.

What Justification is Not
1. Justification is not a case of God pronouncing us righteous because we are innocent, good or decent, but even though we are sinners.
2. Justification is not by our works or efforts, a case of making ourselves righteous by reforming ourselves; it is not 'turning over a new leaf'.
3. Justification is not a case of God *making* us righteous, for we remain sinners in practice, but of God *pronouncing* us righteous.
4. Justification is not God giving us His divine nature so that we become righteous (this is regeneration, or new birth). It is not God *imparting* righteousness to us, but *imputing* (or crediting) it to us.
5. Justification is not a gradual process by which, over time we become more righteous (this is sanctification). It is an instantaneous act.
6. Justification is more than being pardoned. It is acquitted, as if the sins were never committed. Justified is 'just as if I'd never sinned'.
7. Justification is not simply a verdict that will be pronounced in the future at judgment day, for we have already been justified now.

How We are Justified
1.   We are not Justified by the works of the law: 'By the deeds of the law, no flesh will be justified in His sight' (Rom. 3:20).
2.   We are not Justified by birth: 'there is One God who will justify the circumcised by faith and the uncircumcised through faith' (Rom. 3:30).
3.   We are Justified by God's grace: 'Being justified freely by His grace through the redemption that is in Christ Jesus' (Romans 3:24).
4.   We are Justified by Christ's blood: 'Having now been justified by His blood, we shall be saved from wrath through Him' (Romans 5:9).
5.   We are Justified by Faith: 'Therefore we conclude that a man is justified by faith apart from the deeds of the law' (Romans 3:28).

Results of Jusification
1. We have peace with God (Rom. 5:1).
2. We are reconciled to God (Rom. 5:10).
3. There is no condemnation (Rom. 8:1).
4. We have eternal life (Rom. 5:18, 21).
5. We have the very righteousness of God himself (2 Cor. 5:21).

47 NEW BIRTH

George Whitefield was born in a pub in England in 1714. When he was a teenager, he became decidedly religious. He said his prayers and sang psalms three times a day, visited the poor, fasted on Fridays, and received communion once a month. At university, he redoubled his efforts to be religious. Then one day, he found a book that said that religion does not consist in good deeds but in being born again. Whitefield tried even harder to be born again: he ceased laughing, gave up his friends, prayed in the cold and rain, ate no pleasant food, and did not worry about dressing respectably. But still he had no peace, no joy – and no new birth. A little while later he visited the jail and read John 3 to a prisoner and his wife who had just tried to commit suicide. As he read verse 16, the woman burst out that she believed and had been born again, and then her husband said so too. Whitefield was shocked that sinful people could be born again, when he was not. He struggled on until, weak with sickness, he called out to God to save him, and put his trust in Christ's death upon the cross. He went on to become one of the greatest gospel preachers in the English-speaking world, and one of his favourite sermons was on John 3, and the need to be born again.

What being Born Again does NOT mean

Being born again is, at first, a strange idea. Nicodemus did not understand what Jesus meant by this idea (John 3:7). It does **not** mean:

1. **Reincarnation**: The Bible does not teach that after you die you are reborn again in another life. We only die once (Heb. 9:27).
2. **Religion**: being born again does not mean getting all religious. It is not something you do at all, but something that God does.
3. **Reinvention**: being born again does not mean reforming yourself, or making changes. It when God changes you from the inside out.

What being Born Again means

Being born again means to be born of God (John 1:12-13), born from above, becoming a child of God. We are born again spiritually, becoming part of God's family. Being born again is also called regeneration.

Why do we need to be Born again?
Unless we are born again, we will not see the kingdom of God (John 3:3), or be in heaven. Only members of God's family rightly belong in God's house. To be in God's family we have to share God's nature, but our problem is that we do not share God's nature. We are sinners, while He is holy. Thus, we have to be born again.

Who Needs to be Born again?
Jesus told Nicodemus he needed to be born again, despite the fact he was (a) a Pharisee – very religious, (b) a ruler – respected in the community, (c) a teacher – a Rabbi, and (d) a Jew – one of the chosen race. If even Nicodemus, one of the best of men, was not going to be in heaven, but needed to be born again, then all people need to be born again.

What does Christ mean by being born of water and spirit (John 3:5)?
There are three main suggestions: water refers (A) to baptism, (B) to the Word of God, or (C) to the Holy Spirit. Many churches teach baptismal regeneration based on (A), however the Bible repeatedly teaches that we are saved by faith in Christ, not baptism (Rom. 10:9). It is doubtful that water refers to the Word of God here, despite Eph. 5:26, 1 Peter 1:23 and Jam. 1:18, which teach we are born again through the Word of God, for Jesus makes no mention of the Word of God in the context. John's Gospel instead uses water as a symbol of cleansing (John 2:6, 3:25) and of the Holy Spirit (John 4:10-14, 7:37-39). Ezek. 36:25-28 promises new birth: sprinkling clean water on Israel, cleansing them from their sins, giving them a new heart, putting a new spirit within, and making them God's people. In Ezekiel, water speaks of cleansing from sin, while spirit refers to new life. Tit. 3:5 links washing of new birth and renewing of (i.e. by) the Holy Spirit (cf. 1 Cor. 6:11).

How are we Born again?
In John 3:11-16, Jesus describes how the new birth happens. Five times, Jesus uses the words 'receive' and 'believe'. This is what we have to do to be born again – we receive Christ, we believe in Him (see also John 1:12), putting our trust in Christ as our Saviour. John 3:15-16 say that whoever believes in Him shall not perish but have everlasting life.

48 FAITH

The Bible teaches that we are saved through faith (John 3:16, Acts 10:43, 16:30-31, Rom. 10:9, Eph. 2:8, etc.). But what exactly is faith?

Wrong Ideas about Faith
1. Atheists think that faith is 'blind trust', or that faith is 'belief in the absence of evidence'.
2. Some non-Christians speak of faith as a mystical gift ('I wish I had your faith').
3. 'Word of Faith' Christians say that faith is a powerful, creative force.

Faith involves Four Things
W. H. Griffith-Thomas' definition: Faith 'affects the whole of man's nature. It commences with the **conviction** *of the mind* based on adequate evidence; it continues in the **confidence** *of the heart* or emotions based on conviction, and it is crowned in the **consent** *of the will*, by means of which the conviction and confidence are *expressed in* **conduct**[49].

The girl who asked her father to build a doll's house, and then started getting her dolls and toys ready for it, illustrates faith: she was convinced, she trusted (had confidence in) her father, her faith was seen in conduct (action), and all action results from a choice of the will (consent).

HEBREWS 11 – THE BIBLE'S DEFINITION OF FAITH
1. Faith involves **Conviction**. Faith or belief is being sure (Heb. 11:1, NIV), convinced, or fully persuaded of something. It is the opposite of doubt, it is 'full assurance of faith' (Heb. 10:22, and see 1 Thess. 1:5 and Rom. 4:21). Griffith-Thomas' definition of faith involved 'conviction of mind based on adequate evidence'. Is there adequate evidence for the Christian faith or is Christian faith a leap in the dark? The Christian faith is based primarily upon the death and resurrection of Jesus, events for which there is strong and compelling historical evidence that people may investigate. The idea that Christianity is a blind leap in the dark is baseless nonsense.
2. Faith involves **Confidence**. Faith is being sure of things **hoped** for and certain of things **not seen** (Hebrews 11:1). Faith involves trusting

God about things He has promised, things that we cannot yet see, and sometimes things we don't fully understand. Faith involves an element in which we step out into the unknown, trusting that underfoot we will find solid rock. Faith is 'reasonable trust'; that is, faith involves convictions based on good reasons, but it also involves the further step of commitment. The usual OT word for faith is trust. See examples of this in Hebrews 11: Noah (v7), Abraham (v8). Belief in God involves trusting Him to keep His Word and its promises (e.g. about His pardon, eternal life.)
3. Faith is expressed in **Conduct**. People's actions (or lack thereof) show whether they believe something. Hebrews 11 is full of people who acted on their faith (e.g. Abraham, v8). Faith cannot be passive, or simply give verbal assent to some idea. True faith takes action.
4. Faith involves **Consent** of the will. Faith involves a decision or choice. Thus, 'By faith Moses ... refused to be called the son of Pharaoh's daughter, choosing rather to suffer affliction with the people of God than to enjoy the pleasures of sin ...' (Heb. 11:24-26).

How Do We Believe?

We hear with our ears: 'faith comes by hearing, and hearing by the word of Christ' (Rom. 10:17, ESV). We hear the good news about Christ.

We believe in our heart (see Rom. 10:9). When a person hears the gospel, they think about it, and believe it. In Lydia's case (Acts 16:14), she thought about and believed the message.

We respond by agreeing with our mouth (see Rom. 10:9). What we believe in our heart comes out on our lips in prayer to God. Confession here does not refer to confessing sins, or telling other people that we have trusted Christ (although that is good). Instead, when we believe, we cry out to God for salvation, we call on the Lord (see Rom. 10:13).

Becoming a Christian involves three things. I admit that I am a sinner who needs to be saved (Rom. 3:23, 6:23). I believe that Jesus Christ is the Son of God who died for me, and rose again (Rom. 10:9). I call upon Him to save me (Romans 10:13). This decision can be expressed in a simple prayer: God, I am sorry for my sins, I believe in the Lord Jesus Christ who died for me on the cross, please forgive me and save me.

49 FAITH AND WORKS

The Bible teaches that we are saved by faith, not works. Thus, Romans 3:28 says, 'Therefore we conclude that a man is justified by faith apart from the works of the law' (see also Gal. 2:15-16, Eph. 2:8-9). There are two reactions to the idea that salvation is by faith not works:

1. **Faith plus Works**. Some argue that the Bible teaches that we are saved by faith *and* works. While agreeing that we have to believe to be saved, they argue that we also need to add works to our faith to be saved. They quote James' words, 'faith without works is dead' (James 2:26) and point to what Paul said, 'Work out your own salvation with fear and trembling' (Phil. 2:12). The Roman Catholic Church teaches that good works by the faithful obtain merit. Ott writes, 'the justified eternal life is both a gift of grace promised by God and a reward for his own good works and merits ... Salutary works are, at the same time, gifts of God and meritorious acts of man'[50].
2. **Cheap Grace**. Others take the Bible's message of salvation by grace through faith and not works as a licence to live careless, worldly, unholy lives. They think that if we are saved simply by faith, then it does not matter what sins we commit, or how many, because we have an insurance policy that promises us eternal life. These people take grace for granted. Dietrich Bonhoeffer called this 'cheap grace': 'Cheap grace is the preaching of forgiveness without requiring repentance, baptism without church discipline, communion without confession. Cheap grace is grace without discipleship, grace without the cross, grace without Jesus Christ'[51].

RESOLUTION

Neither of these positions (faith *plus* works, or cheap grace) represent what the Bible teaches about the nature of salvation and the relationship between faith and works. The problem with the idea that we are saved by faith and works is that this undermines the work of Christ. If our works could have saved us, why did Christ need to die? Our works cannot save us; instead, because our works always fall short of God's standard, they only ever condemn us (see Rom. 4:4).

On the other hand, true faith is always expressed in conduct; it involves action. True faith in Christ will result in a changed life. It is impossible for someone to believe in Christ and go on living in the same way they did before. Christ said, 'you will know them by their fruits' (Matt. 7:15-16, cf. vs21-23).

Thus, good works do not save, but salvation leads to and produces good works. Good works do not save, but they show the evidence that someone is saved. It is like the fruit on a tree: the fruit does not give the tree life nor even keep the tree alive (this comes from rainwater and the nutrients in the ground), nevertheless, the fruit shows evidence that the tree is alive. Luther put it this way: 'We are saved by faith alone, but the faith that saves is never alone'.

James 2:14-26
James teaches that genuine faith is seen in ***works*** as opposed to mere ***words*** (note the word 'say' in verses 14, 15, 18). James gives examples of people who say they believe, but it is just idle talk. James is warning against a nominal Christianity that merely mouths and parrots the words of creeds. Instead of empty professions of faith, James calls for his readers to produce actions that show real faith.

Philippians 2:12-13
In Phil. 2:12-13, Paul writes, 'Therefore, my beloved, as you have always obeyed, not as in my presence only, but now much more in my absence, work out your own salvation with fear and trembling; for it is God who works in you both to will and to do for His good pleasure'. Paul is again writing about us 'working out', i.e. demonstrating the fruit of our salvation by our works. Notice that Paul immediately follows 'work out your own salvation' by saying that it is God who is working in us.

Ephesians 2:8-10
This passage tells us that we are saved to do good works (verse 10). Our works show our faith.

50 HUMAN RESPONSIBILITY AND FREE WILL

Man was created in the image of God and given genuine freedom, able to make choices between different alternatives.

HUMAN RESPONSIBILITY IN SALVATION

The arguments for human responsibility in salvation are obvious:

- The new Christian has been saved through the preaching of the gospel, which places before them two alternatives: sin or righteousness, heaven or hell, salvation or being lost.
- The preacher's task also implies human responsibility; it involves reasoning with and persuading people (Acts 18:4). The preacher can say, 'God [is] pleading through us; we implore you on Christ's behalf, be reconciled to God' (2 Cor. 5:20). By reasoning, persuading, imploring and pleading, the preacher attempts to win the unbeliever to Christ.
- We must 'obey the gospel' (2 Thess. 1:8, 1 Peter 4:17) by repenting from sin, turning from idols to serve the living and true God (1 Thess. 1:9). We must 'call upon the name of the Lord' (Romans 10:13). Obedience requires a choice. It is our responsibility to repent towards God and have faith towards our Lord Jesus Christ (Acts 20:21).

Several salvation pictures and Scriptures also imply human responsibility.

- Salvation is a gift (Eph. 2:8) – it is offered, not forced upon us.
- The gospel message is an invitation: God calls to men ('many are called', Matthew 22:14); it is our responsibility to respond, but many choose to ignore or turn down the invitation or make excuses. We are told that those who 'receive' Christ (John 1:12) and 'accept' the gospel (1 Tim. 1:15), are saved, and these words place the responsibility upon the recipient to receive and accept Christ.
- 'Whoever will' may be saved. Christ said 'whoever believes will not perish but have everlasting life' (John 3:15, 16, 4:14), Peter preached 'whoever believes in Him will receive forgiveness of sins' (Acts 10:43), Paul says 'whoever believes in Him' and 'whoever calls on the name of the Lord shall be saved' (Rom. 10:11, 13), John said 'whoever believes that Jesus is the Christ' is born of God (1 John 5:1). Revelation 22:17 says 'whoever desires (i.e. wills), let him take of the water of life freely'.

- Other verses stress that the gospel message is for anyone and all. Christ said, 'Come to me, all you who labour and are heavy laden and I will give you rest' (Matthew 11:28). Mark 16:15 says 'Go into all the world and preach the gospel to every creature', while Acts 17:30 says that 'God ... now commands all men everywhere to repent' (see also Isaiah 45:22, -55:1, John 7:37).
- In the parable, the Master said, 'yet there is room' (Luke 14:22). God has room for all who will come, and wishes them to do so.
- Christ congratulated people on their faith (Luke 7:9, 17:18-19, etc.) and says it has saved them (Matt. 9:22, Luke 7:50).
- Men have to choose. Deut. 30:19 says, 'I have set before you life and death, blessing and cursing; therefore choose life'. Joshua 24:15 says, 'Choose you this day who you will serve'. See also Jer. 21:8.
- God's desire is for the salvation of all people: 1 Tim. 2:1-4 says 'for this is good and acceptable in the sight of God our Saviour, who will have (or, desires) all men to be saved and to come to the knowledge of the truth. 2 Peter 3:9 says that 'God is not willing that any should perish, but that all should come to repentance'. See also Ezek. 33:11.

C. S. Lewis wrote: 'God created things which had free will. That means creatures which can go wrong or right... Why, then, did God give them free will? Because free will, though it makes evil possible, is also the only thing that makes possible any love or goodness or joy worth having. A world of automata ... machines – would hardly be worth creating. The happiness which God designs for His higher creatures is the happiness of being freely, voluntarily united to Him'[52].

'Remove free will and there will be nothing to save; remove grace and there will be nothing to save with' (St. Bernard). 'That God's rational creatures, angelic and humans, have free agency (power of personal decision as to what they shall do) is clear in Scripture throughout; we would not be moral beings, answerable to God the judge, were it not so ... Yet the fact of free agency confronts us with mystery, inasmuch as God's control over our free, self-determined activities is as complete as it is over anything else, and how this can be we do not know' (J. I. Packer[53]).

51 ELECTION

Scripture teaches divine sovereignty, that God is the Lord of all things, in control of every event that happens in creation (even the fall of a sparrow to the ground, Matt. 10:29). On the other hand, humans have the ability to freely make choices. How these facts of divine sovereignty and human freedom can both be true is a mystery. But we see it in various examples from biblical history:
- Prophecy: is the future path of history running to the plan of fate, or is it the result of free decisions of man?
- Was Judas prophesied to betray Jesus, or could Judas have chosen not to betray Jesus?
- Christ's death: Acts 2:23 - 'him being delivered by the determined purpose and foreknowledge of God, you have taken by lawless hands, have crucified, and put to death'.

DIVINE ELECTION IN SALVATION

Election means choosing certain people out of a greater number. God chose certain people to be saved before time began. NT references:
- In Romans 8:33, we are called the 'elect of God'; see also Col. 3:12 ('God's chosen ones', ESV), 1 Thess. 1:4, Titus 1:1, 2 Peter 1:10.
- 2 Thess. 2:13 says 'we are bound to give thanks to God always for you, brethren beloved of the Lord, because God from the beginning chose you for salvation through sanctification by the Spirit and belief in the truth, to which he called you by our gospel, for the obtaining of the glory of our Lord Jesus Christ'. This verse does not say that the Thessalonians chose God for salvation, nor is it saying that God chose salvation for them, but that God chose them to be saved.
- Ephesians 1:4-5 says, 'He chose us in Him before the foundation of the world that we should be holy and without blame before Him, in love having predestined us to adoption as sons by Jesus Christ to Himself'. Note: 'God chose *us* for salvation', not 'God chose salvation for us'. Being 'predestined' means we were destined before the world to be adopted.
- Acts 13:48, 'as many as had been appointed to eternal life believed'.
- We are blind (2 Cor. 4:4); God must open our eyes (2 Cor. 4:6).

- Salvation is 'new birth'; John 1:12-13 says we were born 'not of blood, nor of the will of the flesh, nor of the will of man, but of God'.
- We were 'dead' before we were saved (in 'trespasses and sins', Eph. 2:1; John 5:21, 5:24, 1 John 3:14). The dead cannot rise to life – this requires God's miracle of new life.
- Romans 3:11 says that as part of our sinful condition, 'there is none who seeks after God'. John 6:44 explains how we are saved: 'No one can come to me unless the Father who sent me draws him'.

OBJECTIONS

Foreknowledge (Rom. 8:29-30, 1 Pet. 1:2). Some argue that God chose those who He knew would believe the gospel. However, this robs the word 'choose' of any meaning, for God did not really choose at all. It is like Communist 'democracy', the choice people had when they had no choice. Foreknowledge involves more than just knowing the future, rather 'foreordaining' (1 Pet. 1:20 Gr., cf. 1 Pet. 1:2, Acts 2:23, Rom. 11:2, 5, 28). God knew and chose individuals before time (Jer. 1:5).

Corporate Election: Some argue that God did not choose individuals to be saved, but the church. But the Bible never puts it this way. In any case, choosing a team always involves choosing the individuals who make it up.

Moral: Some object it is not fair for God to choose some to be saved. But God is not being unfair to those who are not saved, for they receive what their sins deserve. God is not obligated to save anyone; few complain that God has not provided salvation for the demons. God, in grace, gives more than what we deserve to whom He wishes (see Rom. 9:15-16).

Practical: Does not God's election mean that, since He knows who will be saved, there is no point in preaching the gospel? No, for divine election does not remove human responsibility, either for the sinner to repent and believe the gospel, or for the saint to preach it. Some of the most energetic evangelists have believed strongly in election.

How do we reconcile election and free will? The truth is not in one extreme, nor in the middle, but in both extremes (A. P. Gibbs, quoting Charles Simeon). Both divine sovereignty and human responsibility are true. Jesus said, 'All that the Father gives Me will come to Me, and the one who comes to Me I will by no means cast out' (John 6:37).

52 ETERNAL SECURITY

FALLING AWAY FROM FAITH

Cases of people 'falling away' from faith are found in the Bible:

- Judas, one of Jesus' closest followers, turned away from Christ and literally sold out his faith.
- Some 'believe for a while, and in time of temptation fall away' (Luke 8:13). Others turn from God back to sin (2 Pet. 2:20-22).
- In 1 Tim. 4:1, we read 'in latter times some will depart from the faith, giving heed to deceiving spirits and doctrines of demons' (1 Tim. 4:1, and see 2 Tim. 2:17-18)
- There are also verses in the New Testament which make salvation conditional upon people 'holding fast' and 'continuing in the faith': 1 Cor. 15:1-2, Col. 1:21-23, Heb. 3:6, 14.

Thus, some people believe in the 'falling away' doctrine. They argue that ideas of 'once saved, always saved' only encourage carelessness and complacency. Christians instead need to be warned that only those who 'endure to the end will be saved' (Matt.0:22).

ETERNAL SECURITY

On the other hand, many Bible verses teach a believer can never lose his or her salvation. In John 10:27-29, Christ says, 'I give [my sheep] eternal life and they shall never perish, neither shall anyone snatch them out of my hand'. In John 17:11-15, Christ prays, 'Father keep them'. In Phil. 1:6, Paul writes, 'He who has begun a good work in you will complete it until the day of Jesus Christ'. Similarly, in 1 Cor. 1:4-9, we read that Christ 'will also confirm you to the end ... God is faithful'. Romans 8:28-30 teaches that 'whom He justified, these He also glorified'. Heb. 7:25 says, 'He is able to save to the uttermost those who come to God through Him'. 1 Pet. 1:5 says there is an 'inheritance ... reserved in heaven for you, who are kept by the power of God'. Jude 1:1 speaks of those 'who are called ... and preserved in Jesus Christ'.

There are also various pictures of eternal security:

- Salvation is a gift; it cannot be taken away – a gift is 'for keeps'.

- We were born of God (John 1:12); a child once born, can never cease to be a part of that family.
- The Church is the bride of Christ. Is it possible that Christ could divorce part of His bride?
- We are part of Christ's flock – is it possible to stray beyond the care of the Great Shepherd?
- We are sealed with God's Spirit – we are His possession (Eph. 1:13).
- We are the elect: 'Who shall bring a charge against God's elect?' (Romans 8:33).
- Who shall separate us from the love of Christ (Romans 8:35)? Nothing changes His love.

Our salvation is an 'eternal salvation' (Hebrews 5:9) – we have everlasting life' (John 6:47). From a practical point of view, if our salvation were not eternally secure, the result would be continual anxiety and a lack of assurance. John Macarthur: 'If you could lose your salvation, you would'.

HOW DO WE RESOLVE THE PROBLEM?

There are three different types of people: true believers, false-professors and back-sliders. For true Christians, God saves and keeps, but true believers will also continue in the faith. The Lord will preserve us, but saints persevere in their faith (cf. John 10:27-28 and 2 Tim. 2:19). Secondly, there are some people who leave the faith who were never really in it (1 John 2:19). The Lord warned of false-professors (Matt. 7:15, parable of the tares, Matt. 13:24ff.). Not everyone who appears to be a Christian really is. Third, there is also the back-slider, e.g. Peter (Luke 22:32). See also Gal. 6:1 and James 5:19-20. Thus, in conclusion:

a) Those who are Christ's can never be lost, but they show this by continuing in the faith.
b) There are some who forsake the faith and turn back to sin who were never truly saved.
c) There are also true believers who grow cold, worldly, or fall into sin, but who may be restored.

53 ASSURANCE OF SALVATION

If we were to ask a number of people the question, "Are you going to heaven?" we would probably get a variety of responses. Some people might answer, "I hope so". Others might tell you about their church membership, or the fact that they have always tried to be a good person. Roman Catholics are taught that it is a sin of presumption for someone to say that they are going to heaven.

1 John 5:13 says, 'These things I have written to you who believe in the name of the Son of God, that you may know that you have eternal life'. This verse says we can *know* we have eternal life – not 'I hope', or 'I'll take my chances'. Notice also that it teaches that we *have* eternal life – not 'perhaps' or 'maybe', and it is a present possession, not a future hope.

ASSURANCE IN 1 JOHN 5
Seven times in 1 John 5, we read the words 'we know'. This passage is all about knowing for certain that we are going to heaven. It is one of the great chapters in the Bible about assurance of salvation. This chapter teaches us four things about assurance of salvation:

1. Believe
The word 'believe' is mentioned seven times in 1 John 5. Verse 1 says, 'Whoever *believes* that Jesus is the Christ is born of God'. If a person believes that Jesus is the Christ, they are saved and part of God's family. Verse 13 says the same thing: those who *believe* in the name of the Son of God can know with assurance that they have eternal life.

This chapter does not say we can be sure we are going to heaven because of baptism, or church membership, or our good works. Instead, we can be sure we are going to heaven because we believe.

2. The Son
It is belief in the Son of God, Jesus Christ, that saves, and we can know that we have eternal life. Verse 12 says, 'He who has *the Son* has life; he

who does not have *the Son of God* does not have life'. Eternal life is in the Son.

The Bible does not teach that a vague belief in the existence of God saves, for there are many gods in this world. We must believe in the 'true God', and verse 20 says about Jesus Christ, 'He is the true God and eternal life'. We must believe in the Son of God, the One who came (v6, 20), who died, shedding His blood (v6), and who rose again and by His Spirit gives us witness that we belong to Him (v6). Believing that Jesus Christ was just a good man, or a prophet, will not save. We must believe that He was the very Son of God who became man, laid down His life for us, and rose again the third day.

3. God's Witness

How do we know that believing in Jesus Christ saves? How can we have this assurance? The third element in assurance is God's witness. Nine times in 1 John 5 we have the words 'witness', 'testified' or 'testimony', and they all mean the same thing: it is on the basis of God's 'say so', or God's promise, that those who believe in His Son can know that they have eternal life. We have God's Word for it in writing: 'these things I have *written* to you … that you may know that you have eternal life'. If we are not prepared to take God's Word for it, we make Him out to be a liar (v10). We therefore simply have to put our trust in God's witness.

4. The Result

As a result of believing in the Son and putting our confidence in God's promise, we can know that we have eternal life. Assurance of salvation is not based on feelings, but on trust in God's Word. The feelings of peace follow afterwards, and we must not put our trust in feelings but in God's promise. John Wesley described his conversion: as a man read about 'the change which God works in the heart through faith in Christ, I felt my heart strangely warmed. I felt I did trust in Christ, Christ alone, for salvation; and an assurance was given me that He had taken away my sins, even mine, and saved me from the law of sin and death'.

54 BAPTISM

What is Baptism?
The word 'baptize' comes from Greek and means to dip or immerse. That baptism means immersion can be seen from three passages. John 3:23 says that John was baptizing in Aenon 'because there was much water there'. 'Much water' is necessary for immersion, but not for being sprinkled. Acts 8:36 tells of the baptism of the Ethiopian eunuch: 'both Philip and the eunuch went down into the water, and he baptized him'. The Ethiopian would have carried drinking water for his journey through the desert and could have used a little of this if sprinkling was sufficient. Instead, both men went down into the water to be baptized. Rom. 6:3-4 likens baptism to death, burial and resurrection, suggesting immersion in water is a picture of our burial and new life in Christ.

What does Baptism Symbolize?
- baptism symbolizes repentance (Mark 1:4, Luke 3:8), a person's decision to turn away from sin and start living in righteousness.
- baptism symbolizes cleansing from sin, a ceremonial wash. Ananias told Paul, 'Arise and be baptized, and wash away your sins' (Acts 22:16) . Baptism does not wash away sin; it is a symbol of cleansing.
- baptism symbolizes death, burial and resurrection (Rom. 6:3-4).
- baptism symbolizes being united with Christ (Rom. 6:3-4). We show our likeness to Christ in His death, burial and resurrection.
- baptism symbolizes discipleship, a step of obedience to a new master, administered in his name: the Lord Jesus Christ (cf. Matt. 28:19),
- baptism is associated in the New Testament with faith (Mark 16:16, etc.), and came to symbolize a person's step of faith in Christ.
- baptism is a symbol of conversion. It was a ceremony by which someone symbolized that they had become a Christian.

Why Should we be Baptized?
We should be baptized because Christ and the apostles commanded it (Matt. 28:19, Acts 10:48), as an outward evidence of our faith and repentance. Some Christian denominations teach baptismal

regeneration, that is, a person is born again by baptism. However, evidence that baptism does not save is seen in:
- verses which speak of salvation by faith without mention of baptism (John 3:16, Acts 16:30-31, Rom. 10:9, etc.).
- the thief on the cross (Luke 23:43) who went to Paradise without being baptized.
- Paul's words: 'Christ did not send me to baptize, but to preach the gospel' (1 Cor. 1:17), but if baptism were necessary for salvation, Paul could not have said this.
- Cornelius received the Spirit before being baptized (Acts 10:44-48).

Verses used to promote the idea that baptism saves include:
- Mark 16:16: 'he who believes and is baptized shall be saved, but he who does not believe will be condemned'. While both belief and baptism are exhorted (the verse does not say, 'Believe and do *not* be baptized'), belief is given a higher place than baptism, for it is only disbelief that condemns. The NT does not contemplate unbaptized believers, but this verse stops short of condemning believers who are not baptized.
- In Acts 2:38 Peter says, 'Repent and let every one of you be baptized in the name of Jesus Christ for the forgiveness of sins and you shall receive the gift of the Holy Spirit'. Faith is assumed here, for (a) the listeners were 'cut to the heart', i.e. convicted of the truth, v37, (b) those who *believed* were baptized (v41), and (c) repentance presupposes faith. Peter calls on his hearers to show outward evidence of true faith, by repentance and baptism. Other 'salvation' verses in Acts do not mention baptism (3:19, 10:43, 15:11, 16:31). Faith is what saves, not baptism.
- John 3:5 (see under the chapter on New Birth).

Who is Baptized?
Believers are baptized; the book of Acts repeatedly tells of people believing and being baptized shortly after (Acts 2:41, 8:12, 36, 9:18, 10:17, 16:15, 33, 18:8). Nowhere are we told that infants are baptized. The idea that baptism is the equivalent of OT circumcision is true (Col. 2:11-12), but in the NT, a person becomes a member of God's family through new birth, not natural birth, and baptism follows after.

SECTION EIGHT:

The Doctrine of Sanctification

55 SANCTIFICATION

Sanctification means 'the act or process of being set apart or made holy'. There are three ways in which sanctification happens in the NT:
1. **Preparational:** the Holy Spirit sets people apart, under conviction of sin and the truth, leading to salvation (2 Thess. 2:13, 1 Pet. 1:2).
2. **Positional:** all believers are saints, holy in God's sight through faith in Christ. Thus, ordinary Christians are called saints four times in the book of Acts (Acts 9:13, 32, 41, 26:10), while 'the saints' is the normal way Paul addresses Christians in his letters (Rom. 1:7, 2 Cor. 1:1, Eph. 1:1, Phil. 1:1, Col. 1:2). 1 Cor. 1:2 says that 'all who in every place call on the name of Jesus Christ our Lord' are saints – even the Corinthian Christians, despite their many sins and failures.
3. **Practical**: God also calls His people to live a holy lifestyle. 'As He who called you is holy, you also be holy in all your conduct, because it is written, "Be holy, for I am holy"' (1 Pet. 1:15-16).

Contrary to what the NT says about all Christians being saints, the Roman Catholic church teaches that only exceptionally holy Christians are saints. Once the Pope has officially declared someone a saint, they are venerated and prayed to. However, the Bible teaches all believers are saints, and never says we should pray to saints, dead or alive.

Practical sanctification (the third sense above) involves 'striving against sin' (Heb. 12:4), 'denying ungodliness and worldly lusts' (Tit. 2:14), and pursuing 'holiness, without which no one will see God' (Heb. 12:14). We are to 'cleanse ourselves from all filthiness of the flesh and spirit, perfecting holiness in the fear of God' (2 Cor. 7:1). Sanctification is an ongoing process, whereas justification is a once-for-all act; sanctification is a moral struggle, while justification is a legal fact.

Christian Perfection

John Wesley taught Christian Perfection, arguing we are to 'walk just as (Christ) also walked' (1 John 2:6), be cleansed 'from all filthiness of flesh and spirit' (2 Cor. 7:2), and be 'perfect as our Father in heaven is perfect'

(Matt. 5:48). Wesley's idea of Christian perfection involved (1) 'deliverance from all sin', (2) received by faith, (3) given instantaneously, (4) to be enjoyed not at death, but in the present[54]. However, while likeness to Christ and avoidance of sin are the aim and ideal, the Bible does not teach sinless perfection. 1 John 1:8 says, 'If we say we have no sin, we deceive ourselves and the truth is not in us'. This verse is not referring to sins committed before conversion (as Wesley taught), but after, for a few verses later, John continues: 'My little children, these things I write to you, so that you may not sin. And if anyone sins, we have an Advocate with the Father, Jesus Christ the righteous' (1 John 2:1). James says, 'we all stumble in many things' (Jam. 3:2). Paul describes his struggle with sin in Rom. 7 (see vs18-24).

Not only is Scripture against the idea of sinless perfection, but so is experience. Wesley himself was provoked to say some less than holy things to his wife, with whom he had a terrible relationship. A second practical problem is seen in the life of Harry Ironside who, after conversion, joined the Salvation Army, an outgrowth of Wesleyan Methodism. It constantly encouraged people to seek this 'second blessing'. Ironside as a young Christian eagerly longed for the 'second blessing' and finally, one day, determined to get it, went out into a field and prayed in agony for hours until he fainted. After this, a feeling of peace and joy came over him and he claimed the blessing. He announced to all that sin was gone and perfect holiness had taken its place. However, he found himself still struggling with the same sins as before. Evidently his sinful nature had not been eradicated, and he was filled with doubts, fears and guilt. He sought for the blessing again, and proclaimed himself perfect. But he was living a lie, calling himself perfect while he struggled with sins. Other officers had lost their minds, and some had rejected faith in God altogether, saying the Bible was a sham, promising sinlessness. Burned out, Ironside resigned from the Salvation Army and was sent to a rest home full of others with the same struggles. Here he almost gave up on God entirely, but was delivered by reading a tract that said that the Bible did not teach the 'second blessing' or sinless perfection. He went on to become a great Bible teacher.

56 CONSECRATION

Is the Christian life one long struggle or is there a shortcut to success?

The Keswick Movement (1875 – 1925)
The Keswick movement (also known as the Higher Life, Deeper Life or Victorious Life Movement), taught that most Christians are living in defeat, and that the solution to this problem is a crisis of consecration, a step of sanctification, involving surrender and faith. The Keswick conference, held over five days, followed a set format:
- Day One: the problem of sin and spiritual defeat
- Day Two: the solution – sanctification by faith
- Day Three: the crisis of consecration that produces spiritual victory
- Day Four: Spirit-filling
- Day Five: Christian service

Keswick slogans like 'let go and let God', and 'stop trying and start trusting' suggested that an effortless surrender of faith led to a life of victory, without 'known sin'. However, the Higher Life movement had similar problems to Christian Perfection:
- the idea that there is some magic, quick-fix to the problem of sin,
- two-tiered Christianity (the saved and the surrendered, the defeated and the victorious, those trusting Christ as Saviour and those yielded to Him as Lord),
- disillusionment for those who 'got it' when they found they kept on sinning, and frustration for those who still hadn't entered in.

Hannah Whitall Smith's 1875 book, *The Christian's Secret of a Happy Life*, was a 'classic' of the Higher Life movement. It taught that the Christian life is like someone clinging to a rope down a deep, dark well. All the person has to do is 'let go' and they will find their feet inches off the solid bottom. However, the real 'secret' was that Smith herself was not a happy person: her family life was ruined by sin and scandal, and she herself was beset with doubts and fears, living on an emotional rollercoaster. She eventually came to doubt her teachings on holiness.

CHRISTIAN CONSECRATION AND GROWTH

The Bible teaches consecration: a decision we make to set ourselves apart to live for God. We must 'present our bodies a living sacrifice, holy, acceptable to God' and not be 'conformed to this world' (Rom. 12:1-2). We are told 'to present yourselves to God', not to unrighteousness (Rom. 6:13). But this is not a 'once-for-all' step of consecration[55]; consecration is an ongoing need in our lives. Nor is sanctification effortless; it is a struggle with sin by which we progressively grow in Christ. A better slogan than 'let go and let God' is, 'trust God and get going'.

The need for Christian growth is seen in Peter's letters. 2 Pet. 3:18 says, 'But grow in grace and in the knowledge of our Lord and Saviour Jesus Christ'. 2 Pet. 1:3-11 teaches us about Christian growth.

1. **God's Part**: 2 Pet. 1:3-4 says that God has provided all we need for godliness. He has given to us 'all things' we need for life and godliness, through the knowledge of Christ (v3). We are not missing some special ingredient for growth. God has given us precious promises, by which we may be partakers of his divine nature (v4).
2. **Our Part**: 2 Pet. 1:5-7 says we must give 'all diligence' (or, 'make every effort', NIV). We are actively involved in the process of growth. 2 Pet. 1:5-7 say we need to add (or supply) seven things to our faith: virtue, knowledge, self-control, perseverance, godliness, brotherly kindness and love. Elsewhere, 1 Peter 2:2 says, 'As newborn babes, desire the pure milk of the word that you may grow thereby'. We grow as Christians by reading and obeying God's word.
3. **Warnings and Promises**: In 2 Pet. 1:8-11, Peter warns of the danger of not growing as Christians. We will be barren and unfruitful, not producing anything for God, spiritually blind and short-sighted, not having an eternal perspective, seeing only earthly objects, forgetful of how God has cleansed us from our old sins. But those who grow will have an abundant entrance into God's kingdom (v11).

There are no easy short-cuts to godliness, no special steps or mystical experiences. Christian growth is not passive; we are to actively add to our faith. We must be diligent if we are going to be holy and fruitful.

57 THE CHRISTIAN AND THE LAW

Legalism means living by rules or laws. Is this the route to sanctification?

IS THE CHRISTIAN UNDER THE LAW?

In Galatians, Paul teaches that as Christians, we are 'not under the law' (5:18). Some would argue that Christians are not under the **ceremonial** aspects of the law (sacrifices, etc.), or the **civil** aspects of the law (Israel's laws for civil order), but we are still under the **moral** law: do not murder, steal, etc. Calvin argued that the Law had three purposes: (1) to lead us to a knowledge of sin, (2) to curb human wickedness in society, and (3) to give Christians a 'rule of life', laws to live by[56].

However, the NT teaches we are not under the OT law as a rule of life:
1. When Gal. 5:18 says we are 'not under the law', it is not dealing with civil or ceremonial aspects of the law, but moral. The 'works of the flesh' (vs 19-21) and 'fruit of the spirit' (vs 22-23) are moral issues like fornication, wrath and envy or love, joy and peace. The passage concerns our 'walk' (v16, 18, 25) – our lifestyle and behaviour.
2. Rom. 6:14-15 says we are not under law but grace, and the context is whether 'we continue in sin' (6:1), i.e. the moral law.
3. Rom. 7:4 says we have 'died to the Law'. Again the context is moral issues ('sinful passions' – 7:5; 'coveting' – 7:7).
4. In 1 Timothy 1:8-9, Paul writes, 'we know that the law is good if one uses it lawfully, knowing this: that the law is not made for a righteous person, but for the lawless and insubordinate', etc. Paul says the law is for sinners, not for the saved.
5. The Bible never distinguishes between ceremonial, civil and moral aspects of the law. Instead, the law is a unity (Jam. 2:10), and all must be kept, not parts (Gal. 5:3). The 10 commandments contain moral as well as ceremonial commandments. Sabbatarians argue we must keep all ten, but the NT says that we are not under any.

The Christian and the Law: a Paradox

The Christian is not under the law of Moses. We are under a higher law, the law of Christ (Gal. 6:2): we obey His commands and follow His

teachings (Matt. 28:20). This does not produce wild and sinful living:
1. 1 Cor. 9:19-20, 'For though I am free from all men, I have made myself a servant to all … to the Jews I became as a Jew, that I might win Jews; to those who are under the law, as under the law, *(though not being myself under the law)*, that I might win those who are under the law; to those who are without law, as without law (not being without law toward God, *but under law toward Christ*), that I might win those who are without law'. Paul said he was not under (OT) law, yet he was under law toward Christ. We are free from the OT law, but under a new law, the law of Christ.
2. Rom. 8:4 says: 'that the righteous requirement of the law might be fulfilled in us who … walk … according to the Spirit'. We have died to the law (Rom. 7:4) so that we might fulfil the law (Rom. 8:4). Christians are thus to live holy and righteous lives; but the OT law is not the means by which we live holy and righteous lives.
3. We fulfil the law by serving and loving others (Gal. 5:13-14); we are to fulfil the very spirit of the law (Matt 5:17, 21-48).

Ironside wrote, 'We are not under law (Rom. 6:14). We are neither saved by the law, nor under it, as a rule of life; we are not lawless, but "under law (enlawed) to Christ". We stand firmly by the apostle Paul when he declares, "I through the law died unto the law that I might live to God" (Gal. 2:19). Is Christ himself a lower standard than the law given at Sinai? Or is the latter needed to complete the former? Surely no intelligent believer would so speak. This is not antinomianism, but its very opposite. It is subjection to Christ as Lord of the New Dispensation and Mediator of the New Covenant'[57].

There are many serious spiritual problems with a legalistic lifestyle:
1. legalism leads to empty externalism (Matt. 23:25-26).
2. legalism involves majoring on minor matters (Matt. 23:16-24).
3. legalism causes fights and divisions (Gal. 5:15, 26).
4. legalism breeds bullies and slaves (Gal. 4:9-11, 17).
5. legalism keeps a person immature, under regulations (Gal. 4:1-7).
6. legalism does not produce love, joy and peace (Gal. 5:22).

58 WALKING IN THE SPIRIT

What does it mean to walk according to the Spirit (Rom. 8:4) so that we live a righteous life that fulfils the law? How do we walk in the Spirit?

Pentecostal 'Second Blessing': Baptism in the Spirit
Pentecostalism arose out of the 'second blessing' holiness movement. Its standard teaching is that, while we should not expect sinless perfection, there is still a 'second blessing' for which we should seek, which gives us special spiritual power, the Baptism of the Holy Spirit, evidenced in speaking in tongues. A common Pentecostal illustration teaches that when we get saved, it is like being given a new car. But when we turn the engine on, nothing happens – the car has no fuel. It is not until we receive the baptism in the Holy Spirit that we get the power for Christian life. But if no car dealer on earth would give away a new car with no fuel in the tank, why would God? The Bible does not teach a 'second blessing'. It teaches that every Christian has the Holy Spirit. Rom. 8:9 says that if we do not have the Spirit of Christ, we do not belong to Christ at all. 1 Cor. 12:3 says that the evidence we have the Spirit is not any spiritual gift, but rather our confession that 'Jesus is Lord'. Further, 1 Cor. 12:13 teaches that all Christians have been baptized by the Spirit into the body of Christ – that is, by conversion.

GALATIANS FIVE: WALKING IN THE SPIRIT
In Galatians 5, Paul tells us seven things about walking in the Spirit:
1. **Freedom.** Gal. 5:13 says, 'you, brethren, have been called to liberty; only do not use liberty as an opportunity for the flesh, but through love serve one another'. The OT law enslaved people with its maze of rules. The gospel sets us free, but not as an excuse to sin.
2. **Fulfil the law.** Gal. 5:14 says, 'for all the law is fulfilled in one word, even in this: 'you shall love your neighbour as yourself'. If we live a life of love and service to others, we fulfil the law.
3. Paul warns against **Fighting** in verse 15: 'But if you bite and devour one another, beware lest you be consumed by one another'. C. S. Lewis wrote, 'you cannot make men good by law'. Instead, legalism

causes fights and divisions (see Gal. 5:15, 20, 22-23, 26).

4. **The Flesh and the Spirit.** Gal. 5:16-17 says, 'walk in the Spirit, and you shall not fulfill the lust of the flesh, for the flesh lusts against the Spirit and the Spirit against the flesh; and these are contrary to one another, so that you may not do the things that you wish'. The 'flesh' means our natural, sinful state. Paul warns us that we still have that old sinful nature, even after we are saved. But the Spirit of Christ has also come to live within us. We now have two natures, and they are at war with each other. The idea that we can arrive at a place of spiritual victory where there is no longer any spiritual war going on inside us is not true. How do we 'walk in the spirit'? Notice that the spirit and the flesh lust (or, desire) against each other (verse 17). Both the flesh and the new spiritual nature have their opposing desires. Paul describes 'walking in the Spirit' as being led by the Spirit in verse 18. We refuse to feed the desires of the flesh and instead we are to follow and feed our spiritual desires: prayer, reading God's Word, fellowship, service. This is how we walk in the Spirit.

5. **False Profession.** Gal. 5:19-21 says, 'Now the works of the flesh are evident, which are ...' and proceeds to list nearly twenty sins. Paul warns that 'those who (habitually) practise such things will not inherit the kingdom of God' (v21). Those whose lives do not change, but are characterised by the old sins, are not really saved at all.

6. **Fruit of the Spirit** (Gal. 5:22-23). What does this mean? Fruit on trees is the outward evidence of the quality of the tree. Here, the fruit of love, joy, peace (not speaking in tongues or doing miracles) are the external evidence of the indwelling Spirit. Godliness is the evidence of the indwelling Spirit. Plants take time to produce fruit and there is no shortcut to being like Christ. It is a process of spiritual growth.

7. **Fellowship with the Lord.** Paul uses a different word for 'walk' in v25. Literally the word means to 'keep in step' (NIV) or to walk in line. Walking in step with the Spirit suggests (a) fellowship with God, and (b) obeying what God says. Godly Christians know that this is really what the Christian life is all about – sitting like Mary at Christ's feet day by day, hearing and obeying His Word. This is walking in step with the Spirit.

59 THE CHRISTIAN AND GRACE

Eph. 2:8-10 are some of the most well-known words in the Bible:
'By grace you have been saved through faith, and that not of yourselves, it is the gift of God; not of works, lest anyone should boast. For we are His workmanship, created in Christ Jesus for good works, which God prepared beforehand that we should walk in them'.

These verses tell us we have been saved by grace: God's undeserved kindness shown to us in Christ. The message of these verses is that good works do not lead to salvation, but salvation leads to good works.

Grace Abuse

The term 'grace abuse' comes from Philip Yancey's book, *What's so Amazing about Grace?* From the 1980s onwards, a steady stream of Christian books on the subject of grace appeared. These books were largely a protest against legalism in Christian churches – lots of human rules, and man-made traditions that Scripture never teaches. They not only painted the evils of legalism in lurid colours; they also proclaimed the wonderful message that salvation is by God's grace, and that our acceptance by God does not depend upon how we stack up against any set of standards. Yancey defined grace as follows: 'Nothing you can do can make God love you any more, and nothing you can do can make God love you any less' – a nice slogan, but not a great definition.

However, one unintended result (which these books specifically warned against) was that a generation of Christians swung from one extreme (legalism) to the other (licence). Another way to describe this attitude is 'taking grace for granted'. Instead of living for Christ, it is possible to continue living for ourselves, for worldly pleasures, and for material possessions. The goal of life is to be happy, enjoy worldly success and feel good about yourself. The epistle of Jude warns against this problem, speaking of certain people: they 'turn the grace of our God into licentiousness' (i.e. a license to sin, Jude 4).

Dietrich Bonhoeffer called this attitude 'cheap grace'. He wrote, 'Cheap grace is the preaching of forgiveness without requiring repentance, baptism without church discipline, communion without confession. Cheap grace is grace without discipleship, grace without the cross, grace without Jesus Christ'[51].

The Bible speaks about the real message of grace very differently. Grace is something that should produce a thankful love for Christ that causes us to want to please Him. That means pursuing holiness. Titus 2:11-14 says that 'the grace of God that brings salvation ... teach(es) us, that denying ungodliness and worldly lusts, we should live soberly, righteously and godly in the present age, looking for the blessed hope and glorious appearing of our great God and Saviour Jesus Christ, who gave Himself for us, that He might redeem us from every lawless deed and purify for Himself His own special people, zealous for good works'.

Here is what author Max Lucado wrote: 'Get it straight: Someone who sees grace as permission to sin has missed grace entirely'[58]. A slogan that describes grace in a better way is this: 'God loves you just the way you are but He refuses to leave you that way'.

Rom. 12:1-2 talks about our response to God's grace: 'I beseech you therefore, brethren, by the mercies of God, that you present your bodies a living sacrifice, holy, acceptable to God, which is your reasonable service, and do not be conformed to this world, but be transformed by the renewing of your mind that you may prove what is that good and acceptable and perfect will of God'.

Rom. 8:12 says that we are debtors to God's grace: 'Therefore, brethren, we are debtors – not to the flesh, to live according to the flesh'. Hasn't Christ paid our debt of sin? Aren't we free? Yes, but that means we should have a debt of gratitude. Therefore we should live for God.

The hymnwriter put it like this:
O to grace how great a debtor daily I'm constrained to be
Let that grace, Lord, like a fetter, bind my wand'ring heart to Thee

60 UNION WITH CHRIST

What is the secret of the Christian life? J. C. Ryle, in his book on Holiness (written to combat the Keswick holiness movement) entitled his last chapter, 'Christ is all' (based on Col. 3:11). He wrote, 'These three words are the essence and substance of Christianity'.

What does it mean that Christ is the secret of the Christian life? Theologians use the expression 'union with Christ' to sum up our relationship with Christ. Here, we are going to use the term to summarize the two main teachings of the NT about the Christian life. Firstly, **positionally**, the NT says we are 'in Christ' and are identified with Christ. Secondly, **practically**, the secret of the Christian life is enjoying fellowship with Christ. Christianity is a relationship with Christ. Ironside wrote: 'The secret of Christian holiness is heart-occupation with Christ Himself.... Do you want to be holy? Spend much time in His presence... Then the things of the flesh will shrivel up and disappear and the things of the Spirit will become supreme in your life'.

IDENTIFICATION WITH CHRIST

One of the most common expressions in the NT is 'in Christ' (or 'in the Lord'). It occurs over 200 times and teaches one of the central truths of Christianity: by faith in Christ, we have become one of 'Christ's ones' (a Christian). We belong to Him, and being 'in Him', we are born of God (John 1:12-13), we are 'blessed with every spiritual blessing ... in Christ' (Eph. 1:3), we are seated with Christ in heavenly places (Eph. 1:3, 2:6), we are holy and beloved in God's sight (Col. 3:12), and we will inherit all things with Christ (Eph. 1:11). Not only are we in Him, but He by His Spirit has come to live in us.

Paul frequently writes about identification with Christ. We have died with Him, have been buried and risen with Christ to new life (Rom. 6:3-4, 2 Cor. 5:14-17, Gal. 2:20, Eph. 4:22-24, Phil. 3:7-11, Col. 2:11-13, 20, 3:1-5). Since Christ died for us, we are not our own. We should no longer live for ourselves, or for sin, but for God.

This mirrors Christ's call to discipleship: 'If anyone desires to come after Me, let him deny himself, and take up his cross, and follow Me' (Matt. 16:24, Mark 8:34, Luke 9:23, 14:27, John 12:24-26). Since Christ gave up all to save us, we should no longer live for ourselves, but follow Him.

FELLOWSHIP WITH CHRIST

Because we are united to Christ, we can have fellowship with Him, day by day. In John's gospel, Christ spoke of the secret of Christian holiness, fruitfulness, love and joy as 'abiding in Christ'. John 15:5 says, 'I am the vine, you are the branches. He who abides in Me, and I in him, bears much fruit, for without Me you can do nothing'. Abiding in Christ means we let His words (15:3, 7) abide in us, we keep His commandments (15:10), and we ask Him for our desires in prayer (15:7).

COLOSSIANS 3:1-17

We see the truth that 'Christ is all' in three ways:

Our Mental Life (vs 1-3)

Christian living starts in the mind. We set out minds on Christ (vs 2-3), not on things on the earth. We feed our minds with Christ (being 'spiritually minded', Rom. 8:6). This is called 'the renewing of your mind' (Rom. 12:2, Eph. 4:23, Col. 3:3). Setting our mind on the things of Christ is the basis for spiritual victory in our lives.

Our Moral Life (vs 5-14)

The result, in verses 5-14, is that we put to death sinful habits and in their place put on Christian graces. As Christ died and rose again, so we are to die to sin and live a new life of righteousness, like putting off and on clothes, day by day (v8-10). We are to be like Christ (v10).

Our Manner of Life (vs 15-17)

Our manner of life is to be characterized by the peace of Christ (v15), the word of Christ, singing to the Lord (v16), doing all in the name of our Lord Jesus, and giving thanks to the Father through Him (v17). Our entire manner of life is to be characterized by this one thing: Christ.

SECTION NINE:

The Doctrine of The Church

61 THE CHURCH

What does the word 'church' mean? When some people hear the word 'church' they think of a building used for worship. Others use it to mean a Christian denomination, a particular sect. But in the Bible, the church is not a place of worship, or a certain denomination, but instead the people of God, the congregation or assembly of believers. In the NT, 'Church' means (1) the universal Church composed of all true Christians (Eph. 1:22, 5:25, Col. 1:18), or (2) a local gathering of saints (e.g. 1 Cor. 1:2, Gal. 1:2). The Bible's pictures of the church show that it refers to God's people: a bride (Eph. 5:25), a flock (John 10:16), a body (Eph. 1:22-23), a spiritual temple (1 Pet. 2:5). All people in a local church may not be members of the universal church, for some may be false-disciples.

Nevertheless, a church is not any group of Christians who meet for any purpose. For example, two Christian businessmen meeting irregularly for coffee are not a 'church' because there are 'two or three' of them (Matt. 18:20). Instead, a church not only involves a regular gathering of Christians, but it involves a meeting for certain specific purposes: prayer, teaching, fellowship, the breaking of bread (Acts 2:42).

The Church consists of all New Testament believers after Pentecost
- The Lord Jesus spoke about the Church in Matt. 16:18 in the future tense: 'I will build my church'. Christ also spoke about the Church in the future tense when he said, 'And other sheep I have which are not of this fold; them also I must bring, and they will hear My voice; and there will be one flock and one shepherd' (John 10:16).
- Although the word 'church' is used 23 times in the book of Acts, it is never used once in Luke's gospel (nor Mark or John). This seems hard to square with the theory that the church already existed during the gospels, for why was it never mentioned?
- NT verses speak of the church 'beginning' with the work of Christ and of the Holy Spirit (Acts 11:15, Col. 1:18), of the church being a 'mystery' not made known before (Eph. 3:3-10). Paul does not say Gentile Christians are made part of Israel, but (with Jews) being

made into 'one new man' (Eph. 2:15). The church is a new thing.
- The church is 'built on the foundation of the apostles and prophets, Jesus Christ Himself being the chief corner stone' (Eph. 2:20). The church is built on the foundation of NT, not OT, saints.
- The church has a special relationship with the Holy Spirit. He is the unifying factor in the church (Eph. 4:3), the empowering force (Acts 1:8), the gifting source (1 Cor. 12:4-11), and the indwelling presence of Christ, without which the church could not function. All this means that it is hard to understand the church's existence without the coming, and the baptism, of the Spirit in Acts 2 at Pentecost.

The Church's Relationship with Israel

Although Israel and the Church are similar, in that both are the 'people of God' (Heb. 4:9), saved by grace through faith, and both are going to enjoy the New Jerusalem (Rev. 21:12, 14), yet there are differences:
- Israel is mentioned 21 times in the book of Acts, and each refers to ethnic, national Israel. This, despite the fact that the church is clearly now in existence, suggests the two are distinct entities. Israel is used 73 times in the NT, and on each occasion refers to ethnic Jews.
- Gal. 6:16 is one possible exception, if we read the last 'and' as 'even', taking 'the Israel of God' as the Church. But basing doctrine on odd verses (and unusual grammar[59]) is precarious. It is better to see Paul as speaking of two groups, those who are a new creation in Christ... *and* the Israel of God. As Rom. 9:6-8 shows, the Israel of God refers to a spiritual Israel within ethnic Israel, to Jews who are believers in Christ, not to Gentiles. Paul in Gal. 6:16 specially blesses Jewish Christians who walk by faith, as opposed to legalistic Judaizers.
- References to the 'twelve tribes' (Jam. 1:1) or 'the dispersion' (Jam. 1:1, 1 Pet.1:1) do not indicate that the church is Israel, for these are NT terms used for ethnic Israel (see Acts 26:7, John 7:35). James and Peter (apostles to the circumcision, Gal. 2:7-9) were both writing to scattered believers of the Jewish Diaspora.
- Israel was already in existence when Christ said 'I will build My church' (Matt. 16:18), so the church must be a new, distinct body.
- 1 Cor. 10:32 distinguishes Jews, Greeks and the church of God.

62 THE CHURCH'S MISSION

Ken Fleming, a missionary for 25 years to the Zulu people, wrote 'the mission of the church is mission; the mission of mission is the church'[60]. What he meant was that the number one priority for the church is missionary outreach, however mission must also be church-oriented, that is, with the intention of establishing healthy growing churches. The object of evangelism is not just to see people converted, but to produce disciples who mature as members of the church. John Wesley formed his converts into 'classes' which met weekly for spiritual encouragement, while his contemporary, George Whitefield lamented that his converts were 'a rope of sand' because they had no spiritual fellowship.

The Great Commission
The church has been given a commission by Christ to preach the gospel in all the world (Matt. 28:18-20, Mark 16:15-16, Luke 24:46-48, John 17:18, 20:21, Acts 1:8). When a person becomes a Christian by new birth, they automatically become a member of a missionary society: the church. The great commission involves more than preaching the gospel, it involves 'making disciples', baptizing, teaching them to observe all things Christ commanded. We are not alone in this mission; we have His promise, 'I am with you always' (Matt. 28:19). 'When the Helper comes … He will testify of Me, and you also will bear witness' (John 16:26-27).

The Importance of Prayer
Christ's disciples must have felt overwhelmed with their commission. They were few in number, without education, money or power, from humble backgrounds, and they had all failed the Lord by denying or deserting Him. Worse still, having given them His commission, Christ left them, ascending to heaven. What did they do? The disciples did not start collecting money, or taking surveys, or try some street evangelism. They prayed for ten days straight (Acts 1:14), until the coming of the Holy Spirit (Acts 2:1-4). Realizing their own weakness, they waited upon God for His power to fulfil their mission. Prayer was one reason for the continued success of their mission (Acts 2:42, 4:24-31, 6:4, 13:2).

Effective Evangelism

On the day of Pentecost, the apostles preached and 3000 people became Christians. There are three reasons for their success. It was:

1. **God-guided.** In God's perfect timing (Acts 2:1), and by an unusual method – the disciples speaking in other languages – a crowd was drawn to listen to the gospel. Jerusalem was full of God-fearing worshippers visiting from all over the world, a perfect audience not only to respond to the message, but also to later carry it back to their own lands.

2. **Spirit-filled.** The disciples were filled with the Holy Spirit (Acts 2:4) and Peter's preaching showed all the marks of the Holy Spirit: it was bold, passionate, logical, and convicting. 'God has not given us a spirit of fear, but of power and of love and of a sound mind' (2 Tim. 1:7). We need to be filled with the Spirit to be effective witnesses for Christ.

3. **Christ-centred.** Peter did not preach politics, social justice, material prosperity or how to have a fulfilling life. He preached Christ crucified and risen again, both Saviour (Acts 2:21) and Lord (Acts 2:34-36). He preached that people should repent, believe in Christ and be baptized.

Other lessons we learn from the mission of the early Christians:

- **Personal Contact.** We cannot lead people to Christ without making contact with them. 'The Spirit said to Philip, "Go near and overtake this chariot" (Acts 8:29). When Paul could not preach in synagogues, he went into the marketplace to make contact with people.
- **Good Works.** While we are not saved by good works, salvation should lead to good works (Eph. 2:8-10). Good works soften hard hearts and open ears to hear the gospel (Matt. 5:16, 1 Pet. 2:12).
- **Cultural Relevance.** When Paul preached to pagans, he did not first open the Scriptures, but preached from creation (Acts 14, 17).
- **Discipleship.** Paul's preaching included more than the message of salvation. He followed it up with intensive teaching concerning the 'whole counsel of God' (Acts 20:27).

'The world is a shipwrecked vessel, and it is our job to get as many into the lifeboat as possible' (D. L. Moody). 'Every Christian is either a missionary or an imposter' (C. H. Spurgeon).

63 CHURCH GOVERNMENT

There are three main historical forms of church government:

1. The **Episcopalian** model (found in the Roman Catholic, Eastern Orthodox, Anglican and Methodist churches) is hierarchical, based on the office of the bishop (Gk. *episkopos*) who has authority over the churches in a diocese. This authority is handed down from bishop to bishop ('apostolic succession'). There are three orders of ministry: bishops, priests and deacons, with bishops being ruled by an archbishop. First place among archbishops is given to a Pope, Patriarch or Primate.

2. The **Presbyterian** model of church government (also found in Reformed churches) is based on the elder (Gk. *presbyteros*). In this model, each church has a plurality of elders who govern it. These elders are of two sorts, teaching and ruling elders. These are also higher levels of authority: the presbytery, the synod, and finally the general assembly.

3. The **Congregational** model (found in Congregational, Lutheran and Baptist churches) insists that authority resides in the local congregation (not its officers, nor in any external body). The local congregation is autonomous ('self-governing'). This results in a 'flat' model (as opposed to a pyramid model) of church authority. Whereas in Episcopalian churches, authority resides in one individual (the bishop), and in Presbyterian church in a few people (the elders), congregational churches believe that authority is democratically shared by all the members; congregational churches normally make decisions by voting.

4. In addition to these models, some churches have a corporate model of government (with a CEO), while others have no government.

THE BIBLICAL PICTURE OF CHURCH GOVERNMENT

The biblical picture of church government has four elements:

1. The Church has no headquarters on earth: Jesus Christ is its **head** (Eph. 1:22, Col. 1:18) and the Holy Spirit is His **vicar** on earth (John 14:16-18). Christ is Chief Priest (Heb. 3:1), Overseer (i.e. Bishop, 1 Pet. 2:25) and Chief Shepherd (i.e. Senior Pastor, 1 Pet. 5:4).

2. Overseers (bishops), elders and shepherds (pastors) are **synonymous**

terms for the same people. Compare Acts 20:17 with v28, where the *elders* are called *overseers* and told to *shepherd* the flock, and see 1 Pet. 5:1-2 where the *elders* are to *shepherd* the flock, as *overseers*. Compare the identical qualifications for elders with overseers in 1 Tim. 3 and Tit. 1:5ff.. There are only two 'orders of ministry' in the NT (elders and deacons). Overseers (bishops) were not a distinct class to elders.

3. NT churches had a **plurality** of elders/overseers/shepherds leading their churches (Acts 11:30, 14:23, 20:17, 28, Phil. 1:1, 1 Pet. 5:1, Jam. 5:14). There is no reference to any sole leader, 'minister' or 'senior pastor', either at the start of any of Paul's letters to NT churches or in the concluding greetings. Nor in the NT is there anybody called a Priest (all Christians are priests, 1 Peter 2:5, 9, Rev. 1:6; 5:10, under our Great High Priest, Heb. 4:14). Evidence for monarchical bishops comes from the 2nd C. 1 Tim. 5:17 does not show that some elders *only* lead and some *only* teach, but that some are more active in these roles than others. 1 Tim. 3 and Tit. 1 state that all elders should be capable teachers.

4. Various Scriptures argue for the **autonomy** of a local church. The churches of Asia (Rev. 2-3, not 'the church of Asia') are pictured as seven separate lampstands, not one seven-branched lampstand. The NT nowhere refers to any body ruling over congregations: there are no letters to archbishops or general assemblies. The congregation (not the elders or another body) has the power to excommunicate (Matt. 18:17, 1 Cor. 5:2, 2 Cor. 2:6). This does not mean the elders play no role (they should lead), but the entire congregation decides the issue. Acts 6:3 and 1 Cor. 16:3 teach that the congregation has a right to approve of deacons handling their money. Finally, individual members of a congregation had a right to use their gifts in the church gathering (1 Cor. 14:26, 1 Thess. 5:19, 1 Pet. 4:11). There is no record of voting in the NT; consensus is instead urged. We are to be of 'one mind' (Rom. 15:6, 2 Cor. 13:11).

A Balanced Approach to Church Government

The NT balances government by a elders alongside rights for the congregation. This guards against elders becoming dictators or lords over God's people, and discourages a directionless or anarchic church. It also encourages the training (2 Tim. 2:2) and appointment of successors.

64 CHURCH UNITY

In Eph. 4:4-6, Paul lists seven things that unite all Christians: there is one body, one Spirit, one hope, one Lord, one faith, one baptism, one God and Father of all. We learn three truths in these verses:
1. Christian unity **exists**, and it is primarily spiritual rather than physical or organizational (it is called the 'unity of the Spirit', v3),
2. Christian unity is **endangered** (we are told to keep it),
3. We must **endeavour** to keep Christian unity by being lowly, gentle, longsuffering, and bearing with one another in love.

In John 17:20-21, the Lord Jesus prayed that those who believed on Him might be one, just as the Father and the Son are one. He tells us that Christian unity is important for world evangelism: 'that the world may believe that You sent Me' (v21). Christ also said, 'by this all will know that you are My disciples, if you have love one for another' (John 13:35).

THE SINS OF DIVISION AND DENOMINATIONALISM

Christian disunity is a great sin. A divided Church disobeys the Word of God, grieves the Spirit of God, is a bad advertisement for God's love, and hinders the spread of the gospel. Paul wrote to the church at Corinth to deal with their divisions: some said they were of Paul, some of Apollos, some of Peter and some of Christ. Paul asked, 'Is Christ divided? Was Paul crucified for you?' (1:13).

Just like the church in Corinth was dividing and taking party-names, so today the Church is divided into parties named after Christians (Luther, Wesley), doctrines (Presbyterian, Episcopalian, Baptist) and nationalities. Names unite but they also divide; this is the sin of denominationalism.

Solutions to the Problem of Christian Disunity

Some solutions to the sin of Christian disunity only make it worse. The Roman Catholic and Orthodox Churches have historically maintained that there is only one true Church – by excommunicating each other and everyone else. Attempts at ecumenical federation, seeking to build super-denominations, have tended to backfire because existing denominations splinter into even more groups (some join the new body, some stay out, and some form other groups). The reason for this fragmentation is that, the larger the merger, the more doctrines are diluted and denied. The claim that Christian unity is merely spiritual, not visible, also fails because it does not take seriously the sin of sectarian hostility and biblical injunctions to love and unity among the saints.

The solution to the problem of Christian disunity is two-fold. Firstly, federation, rather than being an answer, must be seen as the problem. The biblical model of autonomous local churches, having fellowship with each other locally yet neither corporately bound together in blocs nor taking distinctive, divisive names, promotes true Christian unity.

The second need is the adoption of scriptural policies of fellowship. In Rom. 14:1, Paul tells us to 'receive one who is weak in the faith', even if he holds different views on minor matters. Rom. 14:3 tells us why we should receive him: 'for God has received him'. In Rom. 15:7, Paul says, 'therefore receive one another, just as Christ also received us, to the glory of God'. Christ also teaches the same truth: 'whoever receives one little child like this in My name receives Me' (Matt. 18:5). The two main reasons for refusing fellowship are because someone denies the 'doctrine of Christ' (who He is, 2 John 9), or they give us reason to doubt they are truly saved by their sinful behaviour (1 Cor. 5). The only other class of person to be dis-fellowshipped is the one causing divisions in the church (Tit. 3:10-11); they too deny true unity. We are nowhere encouraged to refuse fellowship to God's people for other reasons. True Christian fellowship according to Scripture is thus based on life not light, on Christ not a creed, and certainly not on sectarian shibboleths.

Christian unity is balanced by church purity. We are not called to have fellowship with those who are not the Lord's (2 Cor. 6:14ff.), with 'christened pagans' or those denying fundamental doctrines of the faith. We are to excommunicate those whose doctrine (2 John 10) or behavior (Matt. 18:15-20) is not of God. We are to balance truth and love.

65 CHURCH LEADERSHIP

THE ROLE OF ELDERS

Three different words (elder, overseer, shepherd) are used for the same work; each stresses a different aspect. 'Elder' stresses spiritual **maturity** and experience, being an example to the believers and the esteem in which the church should hold him. 'Overseer' stresses **authority** (cf. a supervisor in the secular world). Shepherd stresses **activity**; a shepherd should feed, lead, guard and care for the flock (Ps. 23).

The Appointment of Elders

1. Elders are **Made** by the Holy Spirit. There is a divine dimension in the appointment of church leaders. Acts 20:28 tells us that the Holy Spirit makes (lit, 'places', 'sets') church leaders.

2. Elders are **Appointed**. New elders should be appointed by those who are spiritually mature (Acts 14:23 and Tit. 1:5.), either by a missionary or evangelist in a newly-planted church, or by the existing elders in an established church. The sheep do not appoint the shepherd!

3. Elders are **Gifted**. In Eph. 4:11, one of the gifts of the risen Lord is a 'shepherd'. God sets leaders in the church by giving the necessary spiritual gifts to function as such. There is also the gift of 'leading' (Rom. 12:8) and 'government' (1 Cor. 12:28 – 'administration', KJV).

4. Eldership is an **Aspiration**. Paul tells Timothy in 1 Tim. 3:1 that 'if any man desires the office of overseer, he desires a good thing'. A man's desire to be a church leader is good, not evil; in fact, such a desire is an essential element – there should be no compulsion. What sort of elder will a man make if he has no heart for the work?

5. Eldership is a **Work** (1 Tim. 1:3). 'If any man desires the office of an overseer, he desires a good work'. Being an elder involves more than sitting on a board; it is not so much an office as a work. A man should already be shepherding God's people before being appointed an elder. If he is not doing shepherd work, how is he to be recognized as such?

6. There are **Qualifications** that must be met. These are listed in 1 Tim. 3:1-7 and Tit. 1:5-9. God sets high spiritual, moral, personal and family standards for elders and three outstanding qualifications. Firstly, the

elder must be able to govern – himself, his family, and the church. Secondly, he must care about God's people and God's church. Thirdly, in both lists of qualifications, the man must be capable (and experienced) in teaching God's word. Tit. 1:9-10 requires that an overseer be able to publicly refute false teaching as well as provide sound teaching that encourages God's people (cf. 'able to teach' in 1 Tim. 3:2).

7. An Elder is **Recognized** by the Church (1 Thess. 5:12). The church as a whole has a role in the appointment of its leaders – not to submissively or grudgingly acquiesce with whoever is appointed as an elder; rather the prospective elder should enjoy the high esteem of the whole church.

DEACONS AND THEIR WORK

The word 'deacon' (Gk. *diakonos*) means 'servant'. This word is used in a general sense (Matt. 20:26), but also as a term for a class of 'church-servants' (Phil. 1:1, 1 Tim. 3:8-10). While the Seven (Acts 21:8) are never called deacons, different forms of the same Greek word (*diakonia*, *diakonein*) are used three times to describe their work (Acts 6:1-6). It is not true that anybody who serves God in the church is a 'deacon', for everybody in a church should be serving God in some way. Deacons are under the authority of the overseers, who have ultimate responsibility for the church. Deacons relieve elders in practical matters (Acts 6:1-4), but their qualifications (Acts 6:3; 1 Tim. 3:8-9) are primarily spiritual, not practical. Deacons were to serve a period of probation before being appointed (1 Tim. 3:10). Acts 6:6, Phil. 1:1 and 1 Tim. 3:10 teach that deacons are officially recognized and highly honoured for their work.

PROBLEMS OF CHURCH LEADERSHIP

(a) the Diotrephes syndrome (3 John 9) – seeking pre-eminence and power, (b) the appointment of unqualified/unsuitable elders, (c) shepherds failing to feed the flock, and (d) lack of leadership. Leadership is 'understanding the times, knowing what Israel ought to do' (1 Chron. 12:32, see also Acts 13:36). 'Leadership is influence': an elder's example and encouragement may greatly impact others. 'Leadership is problem-solving', and because most spiritual problems are better prevented than cured, God's Word must be taught, publicly and privately.

66 CHURCH CHARACTERISTICS

The Roman Catholic Church claims it is the true church because it is governed by the Pope. By contrast, the reformers claimed there were certain 'marks' of a true church: preaching of the Word (Beza, Luther[61]), preaching of the Word and administration of the sacraments (Calvin), preaching of the Word, administration of the sacraments, and the practice of church discipline (Belgic Confession, 1561[62]).

If someone wished to join a church today, what should he be looking for? For some, a great church has good music, warm friendship and preaching with funny jokes. But what are the biblical marks of a great church?

The early church in Jerusalem was a great church. They had 'great power' and 'great grace was upon them' (Acts 4:33), there was 'great fear' of God (Acts 5:5), they were held in great esteem by the people (Acts 5:13), and great numbers of people were added to the Lord (Acts 5:14). In Acts 2:43-47, we see seven features of this great church:
1. God's presence – so that 'fear came upon every soul' (v43)
2. Love in action – they were sharing and caring for others (vv44-45)
3. Joy – 'gladness' (v46)
4. Dedication – 'simplicity of heart' (v46), not half-hearted Christians
5. Praise and thankfulness (v47) – not complaining and grumbling
6. Respect in the community – 'having favour with all the people' (v47)
7. People were being saved daily (v47)

Acts 2:42 is key to understanding why this church was such a great church. There are four features in verse 42 that explain verses 43 to 47: *'and they continued steadfastly in the apostles' teaching, and in the fellowship, and in the breaking of the bread, and in the prayers'*.

Teaching

The church is a flock, and the primary need of sheep is to be fed. The church is a temple and needs to be edified (i.e. built-up), so that as we mature our love for one another grows, and the church is *'joined together'* (Eph. 2:21). The church is a body, and its need is sound (i.e. healthy) teaching (2 Tim. 4:3). Christians not on a good spiritual diet become sick and start causing problems. The church is Christ's bride, and it needs to be beautified 'by the washing of water by the word' (Eph. 5:26).

Fellowship

The word 'fellowship' means 'sharing' or 'having things in common'. We see the early church sharing financially with each other (Acts 2:44-45) and caring for needy believers. Hospitality (2:46) was also one of the hallmarks of the early church in Acts, and was directly linked with joy and gladness (v46). More space is given to the early Christians' fellowship than any other characteristic in Acts 2:42-47. Christian fellowship has to get beyond small-talk about weather, family, or politics. It must go beyond mere attendance at church gatherings. Christ has to be the common centre of interest and conversation. Fellowship is the glue that holds the church together. It is love in action (1 Cor. 13).

The Breaking of the Bread

'The breaking of the bread' in Acts 2:42 refers to more than an ordinary meal. It is the distinctively Christian supper, where Christians share bread and wine together, not for physical needs, but to remember Christ. In Matt. 26:26, 'Jesus took bread, blessed and broke it, and gave it to the disciples, and said, "Take, eat, this is My body"', and in Luke 22:19, He said 'do this in remembrance of Me'. In doing so, we 'proclaim the Lord's death till He comes' (1 Cor. 11:26). Why is the breaking of break so important? The Church must be Christ-centred; Christ's Lordship and His work on the cross are given prominence at the Lord's Supper.

Prayer

The early Christians were devoted to prayer (Acts 1:14ff., 2:42, 4:23ff., 6:4). The percentage of people who turn up to a prayer meeting is a good measure of a church. 'What the church needs today is not more machinery or better, not new organizations or more and novel methods, but men whom the Holy Ghost can use – men of prayer, men mighty in prayer. The Holy Spirit does not flow through methods, but through men. He does not come on machinery but on men. He does not anoint plans, but men – men of prayer' (E. M. Bounds[63]).

67 THE LORD'S SUPPER

There are four views on the Lord's Supper (1 Cor. 11:20), also called 'the Lord's table' (1 Cor. 10:21), 'the breaking of bread' (Matt. 26:26, Acts 2:42, 1 Cor. 10:16, etc.), Communion (i.e. 'sharing', 1 Cor. 16-17), and Eucharist (Gk. *eucharisteo*, 'I give thanks', Matt. 26:27, etc.):

1. the Roman Catholic view (Transubstantiation: the bread and wine turn into the body and blood of Christ),
2. the Lutheran view (Consubstantiation: Christ is present 'in, with and under' the elements),
3. the Reformed view (Christ is spiritually present in the elements),
4. the Memorial view (Christ's death is pictured to aid our memory).

The Roman Catholic mass is said to be a sacrifice of the actual body and blood of Christ. However, a literal insistence upon Christ's words 'this is My body' ignores the immediate context in which Christ speaks of 'the fruit of the vine' (Matt. 26:29) after the disciples had shared it (cf. 'this bread', 1 Cor. 11:27). The elements remained bread and wine. Christ breaks the bread as he says these words, thus providing us a with visual, enacted parable of His death, which is also the meaning of 'blood shed'.

Other logical, theological and practical objections remain. Christ was physically present when He said, 'This is My body', so it is illogical to hold that His body and blood were also present in the bread and wine. The idea that Christ is physically present on the thousands of Catholic altars every time the Mass is offered is not true, for although Christ is able to be present anywhere spiritually by the Holy Spirit, yet as a man, He is restricted physically to the one location. The idea that Christ's actual body is continually sacrificed every week is a denial of Christ's completed work (John 19:30) and once-for-all sacrifice (Heb. 9:25-28, 10:14-18, 1 Peter 3:18). Finally, drinking blood is forbidden by the OT law (Lev. 17:10-11). The Lutheran teaching on Consubstantiation denies the idea of a continuing sacrifice, but it similarly misunderstands the metaphor, insisting on a woodenly literal interpretation of the words.

The Memorial view seems correct, for Christ asked us to remember Him by breaking bread; to 'proclaim the Lord's death' (1 Cor. 11:26) shows that the elements have teaching, rather than saving, value. Christ is also spiritually present at the Lord's Supper – not in bread or wine – but among His people (Matt. 18:20, 28:20).

PRACTICALITIES OF THE LORD'S SUPPER

1. **Priority**: the Breaking of Bread was a first-order church activity in the NT, not an occasional event. It was one of the main purposes of the church's regular gathering (1 Cor. 11:17-20). Whether it was held daily (Acts 2:46[64]) or regularly on the first day of the week (Acts 20:7), which was clearly a settled custom (1 Cor. 16:2), the early church 'devoted themselves' (Acts 2:42, NIV) to the Lord's Supper.
2. **Two Purposes:** The remembrance of Christ at the Lord's Supper only occupied part of the church's regular meeting. There was also equal or more time for edifying the church through the use of gifts. This is seen (A) in the gospels where Christ spent several chapters teaching and interacting with the disciples after the institution of the Lord's Supper (John 13-16), (B) in 1 Cor. 11:17 – 14:40, where the church 'came together' (11:17-20, 14:26) for the twin purposes of the Lord's Supper and 'edification' using spiritual gifts (14:26), and (C) in Troas (Acts 20:7-11), where Paul taught till midnight.
3. **Participation**: We read of no minister responsible for conducting the Lord's Supper in the NT. 1 Cor. 14:16 ('giving of thanks') suggests that ordinary members of the church used their gifts in the meeting. 'In [1 Cor. 14] verse 26 Paul gives us a window into the 'meeting together' of this apostolic congregation. He does not say that these elements [i.e. speaking in tongues, prophesying, teaching, psalm-singing, etc.] also occurred at the Lord's Supper (see on 11:17-34), though it is a reasonable assumption that they did' (Barnett[65]).
4. **Preparation**: Seeing ordinary believers are expected to participate at the Lord's Supper by using their spiritual gifts, prior preparation is required. Paul also warns that we should 'examine' ourselves beforehand (1 Cor. 11:27-32) lest God judge us for sin. Personal preparation is essential for worship.

68 CHURCH PARTICIPATION[66]

In the NT, church life involved the participation of the whole congregation. Paul used the metaphor of a body to describe the church in Rom. 12:4-5 and 1 Cor. 12:12-27, with each member having an important role to play in the functioning of the whole. Every member of the church possessed a gift to use for the profit of everybody else (notice the words 'each one' in 1 Cor. 12:7, Eph. 4:7 and 1 Pet. 4:10-11).

CHURCH GATHERINGS IN 1 COR. 14:26-40

This passage is 'the most intimate glimpse we have of the early church at worship' (Morris[67]). Paul writes, *'How is it then, brethren? Whenever you come together, each of you has a psalm, has a teaching, has a tongue, has a revelation, has an interpretation. Let all things be done for edification'* (1 Cor. 14:26). Notice seven points:

1. Paul writes his directions for the church gatherings to the '**brethren**' generally, not to one person (the minister) or to the elders. 'We are struck by absence of reference to a church leader or presbyter. Evidently, Paul looked to a free-flowing movement of the Spirit'[68].

2. **Each one** may contribute, not 'one of you' or 'some of you'. There was opportunity for all (v31) to use their spiritual gifts. Church is meant to be a conference with multiple contributors, not a one-man show or closed-shop ministry.

3. **Variety** of gifts characterized the church gatherings: 'each of you has a psalm, a teaching, a tongue, a revelation, an interpretation'.

4. The purpose was **edification**: 'let all things be done for edification'. Meetings without edifying teaching ('just worship') produce sickly Christians instead of healthy, growing churches.

5. **Guidelines for order** (verses 27-33) ensure variety, decorum and intelligibility. Tongues and prophecy were limited in number, and one at a time. There is no liturgy, or pre-arranged order of service.

6. There is **interaction**: in v30, if something was revealed to a listener while a prophet was speaking, the listener could share the thought. Similarly, in verse 35, people could ask questions.

7. The **divine authority** for such 'participatory gatherings' is given in

verses 36-37: 'the things I write are the commandments of the Lord'. This order of service was not Paul's idea, but the Lord's command.

Church leaders also held meetings for consecutive, systematic teaching, e.g. the apostles in Jerusalem (Acts 2:42, 4:42), and Paul (Acts 18:11, 19:9). However, normal NT church gatherings were participatory, not spectator events. People coming to church 'to sit down and fold their arms and listen, with just two or three doing everything is quite foreign to the New Testament' (D. M. Lloyd-Jones[69]). There was freedom for Christians to speak as they felt led by God's Spirit, using different gifts.

We see the same picture in 1 Thess. 5:19-21: 'Do not quench the Spirit, do not despise prophecies, test all things, hold fast what is good'. 'What is set out in detail in 1 Cor. 12-14 is stated here summarily ... Gifts for ministry were being exercised, but some people were trying to suppress them' (I. H. Marshall[70]). See also 1 Pet. 4:11 ('if anyone speaks').

Similarly, Timothy was left in Ephesus to 'charge some that they teach no other doctrine' (1 Tim. 1:3). Timothy was not the 'Bishop' or 'Pastor' in Ephesus (elders already existed, Acts 20:17), nor did he do all the preaching ('some' implies multiple teachers), nor was he told to appoint suitable preachers or to organize a preaching roster, but simply to correct false doctrine, to admonish unedifying preaching and model good teaching. Paul's letter implies multiple preachers, some good and some not, with freedom to preach upon subjects of their own choice, and opportunity even for those of poor quality, but all being held to account.

On the other hand, women were not to take public part in the church gatherings: 'Let your women keep silent in the churches, for they are not permitted to speak' (1 Cor. 14:34-35, and see 1 Tim. 2:11-12). This was not because women are not gifted (Acts 2:17-18) or godly, but because of their different God-given roles and the principle of male leadership[71].

James Denney writes, 'an open meeting, a liberty of prophesying, a gathering in which any one could speak as the Spirit gave him utterance is one of the crying needs of the modern Church'[72].

SECTION TEN:

The Doctrine of Future Events

69 WHAT MOST CHRISTIANS AGREE ON

Most Christians agree on ten things about future events:

1. The 'Great Tribulation'
Before Christ returns there will be a time of intense suffering called the 'great tribulation'. The NT speaks about the 'great tribulation' in a number of passages (Matt. 24:21, Rev. 2:22, 7:14). In the OT, it is called the 'time of Jacob's trouble' (Jer. 30:7, see also Dan. 12:1). Theologians of all camps hold to the idea of a 'great tribulation' period immediately before Christ's return, although a minority hold other ideas.

2. Israel's Regathering and Conversion
Augustine wrote, 'the following events shall come to pass, as we have learned: Elijah the Tishbite shall come, the Jews shall believe, Antichrist shall persecute, Christ shall judge, the dead shall rise ...'[73]. J. C. Ryle (1816-1900) preached on Jer. 31:10 ('He who scattered Israel will gather him'), listing many OT verses that teach this truth, and stating that the regathering of Israel to its land is one of the two outstanding points of unfulfilled prophecy (beside the return of Christ)[74]. C. H. Spurgeon preached *The Restoration and Conversion of the Jews* from Ezekiel 37, but was unsure which would come first. The 20th century witnessed the return of the Jews to their land and the formation of the state of Israel.

3. The Antichrist
In the last days before Christ returns, Satan will raise up a man to rule the world for himself, the Antichrist (1 John 2:18, see also Matt. 24:23-24, 2 Thess. 2:3-4, 9 and Rev. 13:1-8).

4. The Return of Christ
The Bible teaches that Christ will physically and visibly return to earth. See Acts 1:11, Rev. 1:7, Matt. 24:27-31, 2 Thess. 1:7-10, Rev. 19:11-21.

5. Resurrection
All Christians believe that there will a resurrection. Christians disagree over how many resurrections there will be, but all agree that the resurrection is going to happen at Christ's return. See John 5:28-29, Job

14:12-15, 19:25-27, Isa. 25:8, 26:19, Dan. 12:2-3, John 11:23-25, Acts 24:15, 1 Cor. 15:12-16, 1 Thess. 4:13-17, Rev. 20:4-6, 13.

6. Judgment
All Christians agree that all will stand before God and give account: see Acts 17:31, Heb. 9:27, Rev. 20:11-12, John 5:22-30, Rom. 2:5-12.

7. The Rapture
Living saints will be 'caught up together with [resurrected believers] in the clouds to meet the Lord in the air' (1 Thess. 4:17, see also 1 Cor. 15:52). The Pope seems to believe in it: 'perhaps we are not so afraid of … the Antichrist who must come first … fear of our resurrection, however, we have: we shall all be transformed. That transformation shall be the end of our Christian journey'[75]. Christians differ over when the rapture happens, either before, during or after the tribulation.

8. The Kingdom of God
In the past, Christians have differed over the concept of the Kingdom of God, some holding that it is a present spiritual reality (Christ reigning over His Church, Matt. 12:28, Luke 16:16, 17:20-21, Rom. 14:17, Col. 1:13) while others believed it was a future physical reign on earth (Matt. 5:5, 6:10, Acts 14:22, 1 Cor. 16:9). Nowadays increasingly it is agreed that the Kingdom of God involves both of these two concepts.

9. New heavens and earth
Some Christians imagine that heaven will involve sitting on clouds strumming harps. However, the Bible says that 'we, according to His promise, look for new heavens and a new earth in which righteousness dwells' (2 Pet. 3:13). Not just heaven, but also earth. Rom. 8:21 says, the 'whole creation will be delivered from the bondage of corruption into the glorious liberty of the children of God'. God's purpose includes not only spiritual reconciliation, but the restoration of the physical creation.

10. Eternal punishment
The Bible teaches that there is not only eternal life for those who believe in Christ, but also eternal punishment for those who are not saved: see Matt. 25:41, 46, John 3:36, Mark 9:43, Matt. 13:41-42.

70 PARADISE RESTORED

The idea of a future reign of Christ is mentioned in OT prophecies. Here are eight descriptions of it:

Peace on Earth (Isaiah 2:1-4): there will be no more war, all the nations shall come up to God's house in Jerusalem to learn of God's ways, and Israel will be exalted. God's purpose is that all the nations of the world will flourish as they were intended to. Some argue that this prophecy is being presently spiritually fulfilled in the church, but the church has not put a stop to world wars (v4). Instead, the references to Judah, Jerusalem, Jacob and Zion suggest that it is the nation of Israel in view here.

Messiah's Reign (Isaiah 9:6-7): peace on earth depends upon the coming of God's Messiah, the 'Prince of Peace', the King of Israel sitting on David's throne. See also Ezek. 21:28, Zech. 9:10.

Social Justice (Isaiah 11:1-5): with the coming of the rightful King, filled with the Spirit of God (11:2), there will finally be righteousness and justice on the earth. He will bring the oppression of the poor to an end, and deal with the wicked. Instead of corrupt politicians and brutal dictators, good government will make human society a pleasant place.

Natural Harmony (Isaiah 11:6-9): restoration will extend to the animal kingdom (the wolf dwelling with the lamb, etc.). This depicts the removal of the curse from the natural realm. Some have argued that this prophecy applies to the spiritual blessings of the present church age, suggesting that the lion and the lamb could symbolize a man who was very violent in unconverted days sitting down in church alongside his meek and mild Christian brother. But who or what are the goats, cows and cobras among our congregations? The best way to understand the prophecy is to take the animals simply to mean animals.

Spiritual Restoration (Isaiah 11:9): 'the earth shall be full of the knowledge of the LORD as the waters cover the sea'. Everyone will know God. This is on earth, not in heaven; in the future, not the present.

Environmental Abundance (Isaiah 35:1-2, 6-7): the wilderness, the wasteland and the desert will 'rejoice and blossom as the rose' (35:1). See Psalm 72:16. The Bible prophesies an age to come of environmental prosperity and plenty, not in heaven, but on the earth.

Physical Healing (Isaiah 35:3-6, 65:20-22): with the curse removed (Rev. 22:3), there will no longer be any more bodily disease or disability. The verses in Isaiah 35 could refer to Christ healing the sick during His public ministry. However, it is difficult to understand Isaiah 35 in its entirety as applying to Christ's earthly ministry; for example, Christ did not make the deserts 'blossom as the rose'. The passage requires a yet future fulfillment. Christ's ministry was a foretaste of this yet-future glorious period; Christ's miracles were signs of 'the powers of the age to come' (Heb. 6:5), proving that He was the Messiah who will one day reign.

Birth, Sin, Cursing and Death in Isaiah's Paradise

Isaiah 65:20-22 says that there will still be sin and death in this paradise: 'No more shall an **infant** from there live but a few days, nor an old man who has not fulfilled his days; for the child shall **die** one hundred years old, but the **sinner** being one hundred years old shall be accursed'. There are also mentions of children (playing by the cobra's hole) and the death of the wicked in Isa. 11:4-8 and judgment in Isa. 9:7. But there will be no childbirth, sin or death in eternity when we have resurrection bodies (Matt. 22:30, Luke 20:36, 1 John 3:2). Isa. 66:23 also mentions weeks, months and even Sabbath worship in this future state – but how can there be time in eternity? Thus, the paradise that Isaiah describes does not appear to be the eternal state. Instead, it seems to be speaking of near-perfect paradise on earth before the eternal state. This is puzzling, but we will see the answer to this mystery in the next chapter.

Conclusion

The 'world to come' (Heb. 2:5) will be a place of righteousness, joy and peace (Psalm 98:4-9). God will dwell with men (Rev. 21:3). His purpose – to have fellowship with man – will be fully and finally achieved, and the blessings will affect the whole Creation. It will be Heaven on earth.

71 THE MILLENNIUM

The Millennium (Latin, 'thousand years') is 'Earth's Golden Age', a period of prolonged blessing on earth. In Rev. 20 we read of '1000 years' six times. In this period: (a) Satan is bound (20:2, 3), (b) resurrected believers reign with Christ (20:4, 6), (c) afterwards Satan is released again to deceive the nations, (d) there is one final rebellion (20:7-10), (e) after which, the rest of the dead are resurrected (20:5, 12, 13).

Should we read Rev. 20:1-10 literally or figuratively?
Some interpreters argue that we must not take Revelation 20 literally: it is not about Christ reigning upon earth in a future, literal, earthly kingdom but instead refers to the saints reigning spiritually now. It describes the church age in which (a) Satan's activities are bound (Matt. 12:29) – in that the nations are no longer in darkness, but the Gospel is being preached in all the world, (b) the saints are reigning spiritually with Christ, and (c) at the end of this age Christ returns at the battle of Armageddon. Problems with this view include: (1) NT verses in which Satan is not bound (2 Cor. 4:4, Eph. 2:2, 6:12, 2 Cor. 11:13-15, 1 Pet. 5:8, and 2 Tim. 2:26), (2) the figurative view takes the first resurrection to be spiritual (i.e. new birth) but the second resurrection literally – this is not only inconsistent, but it introduces the absurdity in v4 that people live (i.e. are born again) after having been beheaded for their faithfulness to Christ, (3) Rev. 20 reads more naturally as following Christ's return to Armageddon in Rev. 19, rather than as a second description of the battle of Armageddon (cf. 19:20 and 20:10).

Why the Millennium?
1. The Millennium will vindicate Christ: Christ will receive the honour He rightly deserves here where He was rejected, on the earth.
2. The Millennium will demonstrate God's victory on planet earth. God created this earth a paradise, and though sin spoiled it, God is going to reclaim the world He created and reign even here. Earth's glorious golden age is still to come.
3. The Millennium will reward faithful followers of Christ (see Rev.

11:8, Matt. 19:27-30, Luke 19:17).
4. God will keep the promises He made to His People in the Old Testament: Covenants with Abraham (Gen. 12:2-3, 13:14-17, 15:7-21), with Israel under Moses (Deut. 28 – 30), with David (2 Sam. 7:8-16, 23:5, 2 Chron. 7:18, 21:7), and the New Covenant (Jer. 31:31-34).
5. The Millennium will demonstrate the depths of human sinfulness: At the end of the millennium, after 1000 years of Christ's reign in righteousness, Satan will provoke a final revolt by mankind against God. This shows that mankind is still sinful in nature and practice.
6. The Millennium helps us to understand the eternal state: Little is told us about the eternal state. The paradise conditions of the millennium give us a glimpse.

Who will People the Millennial Earth?

1. The saints will reign with Christ over the earth (Rev. 5:10). Firstly, Old Testament saints will be there (Matt. 8:11). Secondly, New Testament saints will be there (1 Cor. 6:2). Thirdly, Tribulation saints, martyred during Revelation chapters 6-19 will be there too (Rev. 20:4). All three types of saints (OT, NT, Tribulation martyrs) will have been resurrected before they reign with Christ.
2. Saved tribulation survivors will re-people the earth. During the millennium there will still be birth, death and sin (Isaiah 65:17-25). But it is not be possible for the resurrected saints to marry and give birth (Matt. 22:30), or to sin (for they will be like Christ, 1 John 3:2), or to die (Luke 20:36). This means that there must also be other people besides the resurrected saints who will enjoy the millennium. But no unsaved will enter the kingdom (Matt. 18:3, John 3:5); people who worshipped the Beast and took his mark will go to the Lake of Fire (Rev. 14:9-11), not enter the millennium. Instead, there are people who are saved during the tribulation period (Rev. 7:14), and continue to live on into the millennium. God will make sure that there are some believers still left alive at the end of the tribulation (Matt. 24:22), able to enter the millennial period. But not all of their descendants will be sincere believers in Christ, and by the end, many will rebel (Rev. 20:7ff).

72 THE THREE VIEWS OF FUTURE EVENTS

There are three main Christian frameworks explaining future events:

The Postmillennial View: Christ will return to earth after the millennium. Postmillennialism involves a three-step process: (1) The church preaches the gospel, and most of the world is Christianized, although not completely saved, (2) this ushers in the golden age of the millennium with its promised blessing for this earth, (3) then, Christ shall return, raise the dead, and judge the world. Postmillennialism points to Matt. 13:33 (the parable of the leaven, a picture of the spread of the gospel in the world), Matt. 28:18 ('all authority in heaven and earth is given to me', an assurance of the victory of the gospel message), Rom. 1:16 (the gospel is 'the power of God', which must therefore triumph), and Matt. 24:14 (the gospel preached in all the world).

However, the parable of the leaven is not directly explained in the gospels, but nearly all of Matthew 13's kingdom parables are illustrated in passages close-by. Christ's nearby words about leaven (Matt. 16:6ff), and the fact that everywhere else in the Bible, leaven is a symbol of sin, point to the spread of corruption and false-teaching. Christ's power and presence enables His church to preach the gospel in all the world, but there is no promise that all the world will become Christian; there are few who are saved (Matt.7:13-14). The later NT epistles describe departure from the faith (1 Tim. 4:1, 2 Tim. 3:1, 4:3-4, Jude). Postmillennialism is an optimistic outlook, but lacks good biblical support. It also denies that Christ is coming soon – He cannot return for 1000 years.

The Amillennial View: i.e. 'no (future) millennium' teaches that the millennium is now, and Christ's reign is spiritual over His church in the present Church age. Amillennialism argues that the binding of Satan in Rev. 20:1-3 is explained by Christ's words in Matt. 12:29 about His ministry (the binding of the 'strong man'), particularly at the cross, and the spread of the gospel since Pentecost. The two battles described in Rev. 19:11-21 and Rev. 20:7-9 are really the same event, Armageddon, seen from two different angles, and the millennium described in Rev. 20

is now, before Armageddon. The Bible only teaches one resurrection and judgment (John 5:21-30). Therefore, the first resurrection in Rev. 20:5 is spiritual (i.e. new birth) and the second in Rev. 20:12 is literal.

However, Satan is not bound in the bottomless pit (Rev. 20:3); he still deceives the nations (2 Cor. 4:4, Eph. 2:2, 6:12, 1 Pet. 5:8, 2 Tim. 2:26). The normal way to read Rev. 19 and 20 is consecutively; there is no good reason to see the two battles as the same event. Rev. 20 presents two resurrections: 'the first resurrection' (20:5-6) implies a second which follows. To take one figuratively (i.e. new birth) and one literally is not only inconsistent, it presents the absurdity of people being 'born again' after being beheaded. It is true Christ is reigning spiritually in the church (He is its head), however the amillennial interpretation of Rev. 20 does not arise from a normal or natural reading of the text. The problem of the spiritualizing approach may be illustrated by the story of a Jew who asked a Christian whether Luke 1:32 would be fulfilled literally: 'he shall reign over the house of Jacob forever'. The Christian replied it figuratively describes Christ's reign over the church. The Jew said that he also took Gabriel's words about Jesus being born of a virgin (Luke 1:35) figuratively to simply describe Christ's remarkable moral purity.

The Premillennial View: Christ returns to earth again (Rev. 19:11-21) before the millennium (Rev. 20:1-10). The saints will be resurrected to reign with Christ during this millennium over the earth.

Premillennialism argues for a straightforward reading of Revelation, with Christ's reign (Rev. 20) following Christ's return (Rev. 19). There are two battles in Rev. 19-20, separated by 1000 years. After the first battle, the beast and the false prophet are cast alive into the lake of fire, but after the 1000 years of Satan's captivity and the final battle, the Devil is cast into the lake of fire 'where the beast and the false prophet are' (Rev. 20:10). This suggests that the beast and the false prophet were cast into the lake of fire (Rev. 19:20) 1000 years before the Devil. The premillennial view of two resurrections, with the millennium in between, makes more straightforward sense of the words in the passage.

73 DANIEL 9: THE KEY TO FUTURE EVENTS[76]

Christ said that to follow what He taught about future events we need to read and understand what Daniel said about the future, in particular, the 'abomination of desolation' (Matt. 24:15). The prophecy in Dan. 9:23-27 is 'perhaps the most important, not only in the book of Daniel, but in the whole Bible'[77], 'the indispensable chronological key to all New Testament prophecy'[78]. This prophecy is the key, not just to *what* the Bible says about the future, but about *when* future events happen.

The **'abomination of desolation'** (Dan. 9:27, 11:31, 12:11) was an idol statue set up in the Jewish temple by the brutal, persecuting Syrian king Antiochus Epiphanes in 167 BC. But Dan. 9:27, 12:11, Matt. 24:15, 2 Thess. 2:4 and Rev. 13:14-15 point to a future, repeat fulfilment[79].

The setting of the prophecy in Daniel 9 is his prayer for the restoration of Israel from their exile. Daniel's prayer is all about the Jerusalem and the people of Israel ('city', 'sanctuary', 'Jerusalem', 'Israel' and 'people' are mentioned 15 times, v 4-19). We find the words 'your people' (v24), 'your holy city' (v24), 'Jerusalem' (v25), 'the city' (v26) and 'the sanctuary' (v26). The prophecy has primarily to do with Israel nationally, not the church spiritually. **The purpose** of the prophecy is not only the nation of Israel's political restoration, but also their spiritual need of forgiveness of their sins (v24). Some say that this prophecy refers to the church, with the words about finishing transgression and sin, reconciliation for iniquity and everlasting righteousness. But while the Church enjoys these blessings, Israel does not yet, and the direct application is to Israel.

Daniel sets out seven events from his time till the End of time, all set to a timetable of seventy 'weeks' or 'sevens', i.e. 490 years:

1. **A Decree for the Rebuilding of Jerusalem (v25)**: After the return of the exiles from Babylon, the book of Nehemiah shows how this first step was fulfilled in the rebuilding of the city in times of trouble.
2. **The Coming of Messiah the Prince (v25-26)**: Messiah is to come after sixty-nine 'sevens' (483 years), but he is to be cut off, i.e. be put to death. Christ 'was cut off from the land of the living' (Isa. 53:8).

3. **The Destruction of the City and Sanctuary (v26)**: The Romans destroyed the Jewish temple (AD 70) and city (AD 135).

4. **Endless wars to be fought over Jerusalem (v26)**: 'Till the end there shall be war, desolations are determined' (see RV, Darby, NASB, NIV, ESV). After the destruction of the temple in A.D. 70 there is to be continual war fought over Jerusalem till 'the End' (see Luke 21:24). Since AD 70, Jerusalem has changed hands 17 times and the walls destroyed and rebuilt 8 times. Jerusalem is the most troubled spot on earth.

The Parenthesis: there are three gaps in Daniel's timetable: (1) from Daniel till the rebuilding of Jerusalem, (2) the forty years from Christ's death till A.D. 70 and (3) the gap here: wars until the end of time. Rom. 11:25-26 also tells of a gap: Israel's unbelief until Gentile fullness. No one knows how long the gap lasts before the last three events.

5. **A Prince to Come will make a seven-year treaty with Israel (v27)**: A second prince, 'of the people' who destroyed the Jewish Temple (i.e. a Roman) will make a yet-future seven-year treaty with Israel, presumably offering them peace and the right to worship God in a Jewish temple.

6. **Antichrist breaks his Deal (v27)**: 'in the middle of the seven He shall bring an end to sacrifice and offering', ushering in a period called the great tribulation: Jewish worship will be forbidden, he will set up an idol to himself (the 'abomination of desolation') in the temple (Matt. 24:15, 2 Thess. 2, Rev. 13), and persecution of any who do not worship him or take his mark will follow for 3½ years.

7. **Antichrist will be destroyed at Christ's Coming**: We read at the end of v26 'his end shall be with a flood', an overwhelming military defeat 'poured out on the desolator' (v27).

The timetable of future events: a period of three and a half years (Dan. 7:25, 12:7, Rev. 12:14), the second half of Daniel's seventieth 'seven' (Dan. 9:26) is mentioned in Rev. 11:2, 3, 12:6, 13:5 (42 months, 1260 days): the 'great tribulation'. If Daniel's first 69 'sevens' were not symbolic, but were fulfilled literally, we cannot take the last 'seven' to refer to an indefinite period, or the entire church age.

74 ISRAEL'S FUTURE CONVERSION

Many Christians say that Israel has been replaced by the church, and that God has no future purposes for the nation of Israel, except as individual Jews become members of the church through faith in Christ. Luther wrote, 'the Jews, surely rejected by God, are no longer his people, and neither is he any longer their God'[80]. Other Christians believe that there is going to be a national conversion of Israel, a restoration to their land, and a special part for them to play in end-times events.

Will there be a National Conversion of Israel?
In Rom. 11, Paul addresses the question of whether God has cast away His people. He answers, No, and in verse 26, he writes, 'all Israel will be saved'. Calvin argued that 'all Israel' here means the entire church, however, in the verses immediately before and after, Israel clearly refers to ethnic Israel: 'blindness in part has happened to Israel' (verse 25) and 'concerning the gospel, they are enemies for your sake' (verse 28). These verses cannot refer to the believing church. Rom. 11 also tells us when Jewish restoration will occur. The words 'all Israel will be saved' point to a yet-future Jewish spiritual revival and turning to Christ that will happen after 'the fullness of the Gentiles' (v25), 'after the Gentile mission is complete' (Osborne[81]). This will happen at the return of Christ: 'and so all Israel will be saved, as it is written, "The Deliverer will come out of Zion and He will turn away ungodliness from Jacob, for this is My covenant with them, when I take away their sins"'.

How, when and where does Israel's National Conversion take place?
Zech. 12:1-9 describes a future siege of Jerusalem: 'all the surrounding peoples . . . lay siege against Judah and Jerusalem' (v2), but 'the LORD will save the tents of Judah' (v7). This has never happened historically and describes a future military conflict connected with Christ's return; God saves Israel, and destroys their enemies. This passage becomes ridiculous if taken spiritually to talk of the church, e.g. v7: 'The LORD will save the tents of Judah (the church) first, so that the glory of the house of David (the church) and the glory of the inhabitants of Jerusalem (the church) shall not become greater than that of Judah (the church)'.

Zech. 12:10-13:6 goes on to describe the conversion of Israel. Zech. 12:10 says that Israel will receive God's Spirit when they look upon Christ, 'whom they have pierced' and they 'will mourn for Him as one mourns for his only son'. In Zech. 13:1, 'a fountain shall be opened for [Israel], for sin and for uncleanness'.

Zech. 14:1-4 tells us more about the return of Christ: 'the LORD will go forth and fight against those nations, as He fights in the day of battle. And in that day His feet will stand on the Mount of Olives' (v3-4). Verse 5 says, 'the LORD my God will come and all the saints with You' (v5). The result is: 'the LORD will be King over all the earth' (v9). This is a beautiful promise of Christ's return to reign on earth.

Israel's Regathering

Many OT texts tell of Israel's return to their land, texts that do not apply to the return from Babylon, but are associated with Messiah's reign (Isa. 11:11-12, Ezek. 37:21, Hos. 1:11, 3:4-5, Amos. 9:14-15, Obad. 1:17, Mic. 4:6-7, Zeph. 3:14-20, Zech. 10:6-10 and Jer. 30:3-11. There are actually two returns, one in unbelief (Ezek. 20:33-38, 36:22-24) and one after they believe in Christ (Isa. 27:12-13, Jer. 31:7-10).

The Rebuilding of the Temple

Rev. 11 describes a temple in the 'holy city', outside which two prophets witness for God, who are killed and raised to life. Spiritualizers take the temple, and the holy city (v2), and the two witnesses to be pictures of the church. But this is near nonsensical: the church (two prophets) witnesses outside the church (temple) in the church (city). Spiritualizers also take the 'holy city' (v2) to be the church, but they take the city in verse 8 (called 'Sodom and Egypt', 'where their Lord was crucified'), where 7000 people die in an earthquake (v13) to be the world. However, it is clearly the same city throughout the chapter – Jerusalem. It is also hard to see how the church (two witnesses) can be preaching the gospel of peace if they devour their enemies with fire and bring plagues and drought on earth (v5-6). Instead, this passage tells us that there is going to be another Jewish temple in Jerusalem. In this temple, the Abomination of Desolation will be set up: Dan. 9:27, Matt. 24:15, 2 Thess. 2:4.

75 THE TRIBULATION

Theologians from all camps (amillennial, postmillennial and premillennial[82]) hold that there will be short period of intense suffering immediately before Christ returns: the 'great tribulation'. Christ said, 'For then there will be great tribulation, such as has not been since the beginning of the world until this time, no, nor ever shall be' (Matt. 24:21, see also Mark 13:19, Luke 21:25-26, Rev. 2:22, 3:10, 7:14). The 'great tribulation' is also mentioned in the OT in Jer. 30:7 and Dan. 12:1.

Some Christians believe that the great tribulation was in the past, during the siege of Jerusalem (AD 67-70). Problems with this idea include:
- AD 70 wasn't the greatest trouble the world has ever seen; for example, far more Jews died in the Holocaust.
- Christ said He would return *immediately* after the tribulation of those days' (Matt. 24:29). This did not happen in AD 70.
- Daniel 12:1-3 says the resurrection happens straight after it.

Others argue that the entire church period is the great tribulation. But if the great tribulation is a time unlike any other (Matt. 24:21, Dan. 12:1, Jer. 30:7), how can it be a period of time just like every other? Walvoord writes, 'a period of trouble cannot be unprecedented and at the same time general throughout the age'[83]. The definite article, *'the* great tribulation' (Rev. 7:14), shows that this is a specific time of unparalleled tribulation.

Revelation tells us about the period before Christ returns, including the Great Tribulation (Rev. 7:14), the second half of Daniel's 70th 'seven', which starts with the Abomination of Desolation (Matt. 24:15).

The Seven Seals (Rev. 4-7): Seals are symbols of ownership (e.g. in Rev. 7, 144,000 servants of God are sealed, signifying that they belong to God). By opening the seals, God starts to take action to bring human government crashing down, in preparation for His Son's eventual rule. He has the right to rule, by virtue of creation (Rev. 4), but also by virtue of redemption (Rev. 5). The seal judgments involve international war, civil unrest, famine, and finally disease and death. One quarter of humanity dies. The great earthquake (seal six) brings everything earthly to ruin.

The Seven Trumpets (Rev. 8-11): The seven trumpets are blown in response to the prayers of the saints, presumably calling for God to take vengeance against a godless world and to take up His power and reign. The seven trumpets show us God declaring war on the world. Two of the trumpet judgments (the fifth and sixth) also involve the imagery of horses going into battle, again symbolizing war. Four features of the trumpet judgments have strong overtones of hell: fire, torment, brimstone and demons. Here we have hell on earth, a punishment for sin, and a foretaste of what is to come. Yet the earth-dwellers do not acknowledge God nor repent of their sins (Rev 9:20-21).

The Woman and the Dragon (Rev. 12-14): The sign of woman in heaven, clothed with the sun, moon and 12 stars, giving birth to a man-child who is to rule the nations, is not Mary (RC commentators), nor the Church (which is Christ's bride, not His mother), but Israel (cf. Gen. 37, God's 'wife': Isa. 50:1, 54:5-6, Jer. 3:14). The Great Tribulation is the 'time of Jacob's trouble' (Jer. 30:7). This section shows us God's preservation, Satan's persecution, and the deliverance of the nation.

The Seven Bowls (Rev. 15-16): These complete God's judgments, and are again reminiscent of Hell (pain, darkness, fire and great heat), as well as being reminiscent of God's victory over Pharaoh at the Exodus ('seven plagues', Rev. 15:1, 6; with sores, sea turned to blood, darkness, frogs). In the bowls, we are shown God taking vengeance for the blood of His people, who get the victory over the Beast (Rev. 15). God is bringing down the evil empire of Satan's world ruler, the Beast.

Babylon the Great (Rev. 17-18): Hand in hand with political power, there are religious (Rev. 17), and commercial (Rev. 18) forces, seducing people from God. They are destroyed in preparation for the Lamb's wife.

Summary: God's repetitive judgments show His power over earth, sea, and sky. God judges the world with fire in preparation for Christ's reign.

76 THE ANTICHRIST

This is the man who Satan will raise up to rule the world during the tribulation period. The Bible uses various names for Him: the Antichrist (1 John 2:18), the 'Man of Sin' (2 Thess. 2:3-4), the Lawless One (2 Thess. 2:9), the Prince to come (Dan. 9:26), the Beast (Rev. 13:1).

Many have suggested candidates for the Antichrist down through time, from Nero to Napoleon. Others have said that the Roman Catholic Pope is the antichrist. However, Rev. 13:8 tells us that 'all those who dwell on the earth will worship him' (future tense). The world-wide worship of one man has not yet happened. Others argue that the Antichrist is just a spiritual force opposing Christ now (based on 1 John 2:22). However, 1 John 2:18, 4:3 show He is also a literal man in the future. Some writers argue that the false-prophet of Rev. 13:11ff. is the true Antichrist (because he is lamb-like, Rev. 13:11). Both 'beasts' of Rev. 13 imitate and oppose Christ, but we will use the term for the first beast. Note the parallels and contrasts between him and Christ, as seen from his career:

The Career of Antichrist
1. Antichrist will rule the world (Rev. 13:7, 17:12-13).
2. He makes a covenant with the Jewish people for seven years.
3. Has a resurrection experience. Rev. 13:3 suggests it is not a true death and resurrection: 'as if' (and 11:7, 17:8).
4. He is indwelt by Satan (Rev. 13:2).
5. He kills the Two Witnesses (Rev. 11).
6. He causes the Jewish Temple worship to cease and sets up the Abomination of Desolation (Rev. 13:14-15, 2 Thess. 2:4).
7. He will be worshipped by the whole world (Rev. 13:4).
8. An image is made to him, which comes alive; all those not worshipping it will be killed (Rev. 13:14-15).
9. All take his mark, without which no one can buy or sell (Rev 13:17).
10. He persecutes the saints (Rev. 13:7).

The Character of the Antichrist
Antiochus Epiphanes (215-164 B.C.), the king of Syria, set up an idol in the Jewish Temple, the abomination of desolation (Dan. 11:31), stopped

Jewish worship, and persecuted the Jews. He foreshadows Antichrist, who will do the same things (Matt. 24:15, 2 Thess. 2:4, Rev. 13).
1. He is vile and contemptible (Dan 11:21). Antiochus Epiphanes seized the throne when his brother was assassinated, and then later murdered his infant nephew, one of the legitimate heirs.
2. He is cunning (Dan. 11:21, 23). He pretends to be a man of peace, and acts deceitfully.
3. Yet he uses violence and force (Dan. 11:22-23).
4. He is self-willed (Dan. 11:36). 'Then the king will do according to his own will'.
5. He will 'exalt and magnify himself above every god' (Dan. 11:36).
6. He speaks blasphemies against God (Dan. 11:36).

What explains the character of Antiochus Epiphanes, and the Antichrist to come? Dan. 8:24 says 'His power shall be mighty, but not by his own power' (Dan. 8:24). Behind Antiochus was a powerful demonic force (cf. Dan. 10:13, 20). Similarly, the Antichrist is going to be indwelt and empowered by Satan himself (Rev. 13:2). This explains his evil character.

The Contrast: Antichrist is the Opposite of Christ

The Antichrist is the exact opposite of our Lord Jesus, the true Messiah. 'Anti' means 'the opposite' and it can also mean the 'substitute'. Antichrist opposes and substitutes himself for the true Christ.
1. Antichrist is a King – for a short time, he reigns over the whole world. 'Christ', God's anointed king, will reign when he returns.
2. Antichrist has a counterfeit resurrection.
3. Antichrist exalts himself, whilst our Lord Jesus humbled himself.
4. Antichrist is self-willed (Dan. 11:36), but the true Christ was totally selfless. He said, 'I have come down from heaven, not to do My own will, but the will of Him who sent Me' (John 6:38).
5. Antichrist makes himself greater than any god – Christ, on the other hand, as Philippians 2 says, 'being God, humbled himself, taking the form of a servant, and being made in the likeness of men'.
6. Antichrist prospers for a time (Dan. 11:36). By contrast, the true Messiah lost everything (Dan. 9:26), but in God's time shall be exalted (Isa. 52:13).

77 ARMAGEDDON

Armageddon, which is a war not a battle, is found in Rev. 19 and Zech. 12-14. But there are two other passages in the Bible that describe it.

Ezekiel 38-39

Ezek. 38-39 describes a great invasion of the land of Israel from the north. Evidence that this invasion is part of Armageddon includes:

1. Israel will know God 'from that day forward' (Ezek. 39:22). This only happens to Israel at the very end of the tribulation.
2. God has 'mercy on the whole house of Israel' (Ezek. 39:25). God does not have mercy upon Israel until the very end of the tribulation.
3. God brings back their captives after it (Ezek. 39:25, 27).
4. Israel's conversion happens after it ('then they shall know that I am the LORD their God', 'I shall have poured out My Spirit on the house of Israel', Ezek. 39:28, 29). This is Israel's new birth.
5. In Ezek. 39:4, 17-20, the birds of prey feast upon the defeated army of the invader. Rev. 19:17-18 describes the same at Armageddon.
6. Ezek. 38-39 lead on to the millennial reign in Ezek. 40-48.
7. Israel is 'dwelling safely' (Ezek. 38:8, 11), so this cannot be a pre-tribulation battle (Israel is not at peace now). Antichrist continues to protect Israel, the site of his worship, through the great tribulation.
8. This battle is not Rev. 20:7-9. Israel was saved 1000 years earlier, nor would bodies be buried for seven months (Eze. 39:12) in eternity.

Daniel 11:36-45

Evidence that Dan. 11:36ff. describes Armageddon includes:

1. Dan. 12:1 (which follows 11:45 and is part of the same vision) occurs during the great tribulation: 'at that time … there shall be a time of trouble, such as never was since there was a nation'.
2. The resurrection follows straight after (Dan. 12:2): 'many of those who sleep in the dust of the earth shall awake, some to everlasting life, some to shame and everlasting contempt'.
3. Dan. 11:40-45 describes a great battle, unlike any from the life of Antiochus' Epiphanes (verses before Dan. 11:45 describe Antiochus' wars). This battle has not happened yet – it is still in the future.
4. The 'King of the North' in Dan. 11:36-39 does not match Antiochus Epiphanes. For example, we are told that he will not regard any god

at all (Dan. 11:37). But this was not true of Antiochus – he worshipped the Greek gods. The King of the North is Antichrist.
5. Dan. 11:45 describes the 'end' of the 'King of the North'. This was not the way Antiochus Epiphanes died (he died of a fever in Persia). It describes the end of Antichrist. It is not the midpoint of his career.

All of this evidence suggests that Dan. 11:36-45 describes a battle during the great tribulation, which is followed by the resurrection, a battle in which Antichrist comes to his end: Armageddon.

The Battle of Armageddon (Dan. 11: 40-45 and Zech. 12-14)
1. **Background**: the seven-year treaty (Dan. 9:27) between Israel and the Antichrist is interrupted at the half-way point, when Antichrist sets up the Abomination of Desolation in Jerusalem (Matt. 24:15). With this event, the great tribulation commences (Matt. 24:21).
2. **Attack**: in Dan. 11:40 the king of the South (that is, the King of Egypt) attacks northwards into the land of Israel, attacking the worship-system of Antichrist in Jerusalem, and the Jews.
3. **Counter-attack**: this provokes a massive retaliation by the King of the North, Antichrist, who enters the glorious land, Israel (Dan. 11:40, 41), and passes on down into Egypt (11:42-3). This is the invasion of Ezek. 38-39, led by Gog and an alliance of nations from north, west, east, and south (cf. Ezek. 38:5, Dan. 11:43).
4. **Troubling News**: in Dan. 11:44, the Antichrist hears news of a great army from the east that troubles him (cf. Rev. 16:12-14). As a result, Antichrist moves north again into Israel (Daniel 11:45).
5. **The Siege of Jerusalem**: in Zech. 12-14, we read that Jerusalem is laid siege by all nations (12:2). Two-thirds of the Jewish people are slain, and the one-third left are purified (13:8), leading to their conversion at the appearing of Christ (12:10-13:1).
6. **The Lord Returns**: in Zech. 14:3, the Lord himself goes forth to battle. Christ descends on the Mount of Olives (Zech. 14:4), causing it to split. The Jews flee from the battle about to take place (14:5).
7. **The End**: Antichrist gathers all the nations to war against Christ (Joel 3:2, Zeph. 3:8). Christ destroys them (Zech. 14:12-15, 2 Thess. 2:8) on 'the mountains of Israel' (Ezek. 39:4), resulting in a river of blood for 300 km, and the slain are buried in the land of Israel for seven months (Ezek. 39:11-16).

78 THE RAPTURE

Paul describes the Lord's coming in 1 Thess. 4:13-17: dead believers will be raised and living believers will be changed and caught up together with them to meet the Lord in the air. The word 'rapture' (from the Latin *rapio*) translates the Greek word *harpazo*, v17, and means 'to be caught up'. 'In a moment, in the twinkling of an eye, at the last trumpet. For the trumpet shall sound and the dead will be raised incorruptible and we shall be changed' (1 Cor. 15:52). Most Christian groups believe in the rapture, but disagree over **when** it occurs: either before, in the middle, or after the tribulation. Here is some evaluation of these positions.

Pre-Tribulation Rapture (see further in Chs. 79, 80)
Arguments against include the fact that no NT verse says that Christ will come back before the tribulation, nor does any verse describe Christ's coming in two stages. It is also a more recent view (J. N. Darby, 19th C).

Mid-Tribulation Rapture
Christ returns at the last trumpet (1 Cor. 15:52), so the seventh trumpet of Rev. 11:15 must be the rapture. However, a trumpet also sounds at Christ's return at the end of the tribulation (Matt. 24:31). The seventh trumpet brings God's wrath (Rev. 11:18, which the church does not endure). However, God's wrath is not only found in the second half of Revelation (14:10, 15:7, 16:1, 19:15), but also in Rev. 6:16-17 (and if this sixth seal demonstrates God's wrath, so do the other seals in Rev. 6:1-15[84]). Arguments for a mid-tribulation rapture thus collapse.

Partial Rapture
When Christ returns, only those Christians watching and ready, faithful and fit for Christ's presence will be raptured (Luke 21:36, Heb. 9:28, Rev. 3:10). However, 1 Cor. 15:51 says, 'we shall all be changed'.

Post-Tribulation Rapture
This is the view of the early post-apostolic church (hence it is called Historic Premillennialism), and the view of most major denominations:

1. Christ returns at the end of the Great Tribulation: 'Immediately after the tribulation of those days ... they will see the Son of Man coming on the clouds of heaven with power and great glory' (Matt. 24:29-30). Christ then sends His angels to gather His elect (v31) – the rapture.
2. The passages describing the rapture (1 Thess. 4:13-17) and the second coming (Matt. 24:29-31) contain five common features (Christ's coming, clouds, angels, trumpets, and the gathering of God's people). Thus Matt. 24 and 1 Thess. 4 refer to the same event: the rapture.
3. The word 'meet' (1 Thess. 4:17, Gk. *apantesis*) refers to a party going out to greet a visiting dignitary and escorting him back to the city. The church will be raptured and return directly with Christ to earth.
4. Jesus taught His disciples about the tribulation (Matt. 24-15); this suggests the church will go through it. The idea that these chapters say nothing to the church, but only speak to Jews in the future, seems odd.

Problems with post-tribulation rapture arguments include:
1. No verse in the NT describes the rapture happening after the tribulation. Matt 24:29-31 mentions neither a resurrection of the dead nor a rapture (i.e. people being caught up into the air).
2. Instead, it says that Christ's angels will 'gather together His elect from the four winds, from one end of heaven to the other' (Matt. 24:31). The closest parallels to these words come, not from 1 Thess. 4:13-17, but OT prophecies of Israel's re-gathering from exile in Gentile lands. Deut. 30:3-4 speaks of Israel being re-gathered from 'the farthest parts of heaven' (KJV, ESV), while Neh. 1:9 speaks of Israel being re-gathered from 'the farthest part of the heavens'[85]. Thus, Matt. 24:31 is not talking about Christians being caught up into the air, but scattered Israel being re-gathered from Gentile exile to Jerusalem at Christ's return.
3. 'Meet' (Gk. *apantesis*) rarely means 'to go out to escort a visitor back into town' in Greek[86]. The meaning is not required by the word itself.
4. Post-tribulation proponents see the 'great tribulation' as the entire church age, despite Christians living in luxury, falling asleep in church, Christian nations, heads of state, etc. This hardly seems credible.
5. There seems little point to a post-tribulation rapture if God's people are instantly caught up into the sky only to return immediately to earth.

79 WHAT CHRIST SAID ABOUT THE FUTURE

Christ's teachings about His coming are the most important in the Bible.

THREE PUZZLING FEATURES IN MATTHEW 24 AND 25

1. **Signs versus Surprise:** In Matt. 24:1-36, we have a number of **signs** that form a countdown to the coming of the Lord: the abomination of desolation (24:15), the Great Tribulation (24:21), signs in the heavens (24:29: sun darkened, moon not giving its light). Then, we read of Christ's coming in verse 30. The Lord is giving us a sequence of unmistakable signs that show us, in the words of Matt. 24:33 that 'when you see all these things, know that it is near – at the doors'. But, when we look at Matt. 24:36 - 25:13, Christ's coming is a **surprise**, without any signs at all. Noah's day (24:39), the two in field and mill (24:42), the thief in the night (24:43-44), and the parables of the Faithful and Wise Servant (24:50), and the Virgins (25:31) all teach that 'you do not know' the time of Christ's coming; it will be a surprise. Nor is it just unbelievers who are taken unawares by Christ's coming; even true believers like the Faithful and Wise Servant and the five Wise Virgins do not know when He is coming. Christ says, 'Watch therefore, for *you* do not know what hour *your Lord* is coming' three times in these verses (24:42, 44 and 25:13). How could Christ's coming be a surprise when the signs of 24:15-30 provide a countdown to Christ's coming?

2. **Nightmare versus Normality:** The conditions depicted in these two sections of Matt. 24-25 are very different. In the first part of the Olivet Discourse, we have apocalyptic calamities, the 'great tribulation', people fleeing their homes and natural disasters. But in Matt. 24:36 to 25:13, we have an entirely different picture. We read of perfect peace and safety: **domestic peace** (eating and drinking, marrying and giving in marriage, 24:37-39), **economic peace** (getting on with jobs in the field and at the mill, 24:40-42), **sleep** (thief in the night, 24:43-44, virgins, 25:1-13), **normal Church life** (the faithful and wise servant feeding the house, 24:45-51), Christian service (servants trading, 25:14-30). These two sections of the Olivet Discourse involve nightmare during the great tribulation and normality in 24:36-25:30, for believer and unbeliever.

3. **Jewish versus Christian:** Matt. 24:15-31 (the great tribulation) is Jewish, while the section from Matt. 24:36-25:30 is Christian. Notice the following five Jewish elements involved:
a) Jewish temple setting: the 'abomination of desolation' in a Jewish temple, 'the holy place' (24:15, Dan. 9:27, 11:31, 12:11),
b) Jewish geographical setting: 'let those in Judea flee' (24:16),
c) Jewish cultural setting: 'him who is on the housetop' (24:17),
d) Jewish religious setting: 'pray that your flight may not be in winter or on the Sabbath' (24:20).
e) A Jewish gathering (Matt. 24:29-30, the re-gathering of Israel from their scattering among the nations after Christ's return).

Christ's prophecy concerning the great tribulation contains no specifically Christian features, and no explicit reference to the church, but multiple references to Jews. On the other hand, Matt. 24:36 – 25:30 contains Christian parables like the Talents (the 'long time' of the entire church age, v19), the Faithful and Wise Servant (master 'delays', v50), and the Ten Virgins (bridegroom 'delays', v5), but no references to tribulation.

How can Christ's coming be a surprise and yet have unmistakable signs, or be preceded by nightmare and yet also normality? Why does the Olivet Discourse have a Jewish section and a Christian section? To be faithful to Scripture we must hold both sets of truth. One solution is that there are two different comings: a surprise, in non-tribulation, (i.e. pre-tribulation) conditions for the church, and one after the signs of the great tribulation.

Post-tribulation proponents try to solve these problems by denying the signs, or denying the surprise. Neither are satisfactory solutions:
1. Christ could come at any moment because all the signs (great tribulation, Antichrist, preaching in all the world, Israel's conversion) have already happened (Grudem[87]). This does not fit the facts.
2. Berkhof[88] denies that Christ's coming is imminent, for certain signs must precede it. Carson[89] argues 'imminent' means 'in any generation', a platitude that does not square with Scripture: Christ's coming is a surprise, like a thief, 'no one knows'; we are to be ready (1 Pet. 1:5, 4:7) and watching (1 Thess. 5:6), 'the Lord is at hand' (Phil. 4:5, Jam. 5:8).

80 THE CHURCH AND THE TRIBULATION

Here are twenty reasons the church is raptured before the tribulation:

1. There is no rapture or resurrection described in **Rev. 19:11-21** at Christ's return, as we would expect if a post-tribulation rapture was true.

2. The church, the Lamb's bride, is seen in heaven before Christ's return, ready for the marriage supper of the Lamb (**Rev. 19:7**). She is dressed in white, rewarded for 'the righteous acts of the saints' (Rev. 19:8), suggesting the judgment seat of Christ occurs before His return.

3. Some people have to enter the millennium in unresurrected bodies, who are able to sin, die, and have children (Isa. 65:20), who rebel (**Rev. 20:8**). But if all the saved are raptured and glorified at the end of the tribulation (as in a post-tribulation rapture), and no unsaved enter the kingdom (Matt. 18:3, John 3:5, Rev. 14:9ff.), who are these people? There are people saved in the tribulation (Rev. 7:9-17) after the rapture.

4. **Rev. 4-19**, describing the tribulation period, never mentions the church on earth, even though it is mentioned twenty times in Rev. 1-3 and 22. This suggests the church's absence in the tribulation (Rev. 4-19).

5. **Rev. 3:10-11** says that the church will be 'kept from the hour of trial which will come on the whole world'; not just from the trouble, but from the time, the tribulation. This cannot mean that the church will be protected through it, for many tribulation saints are martyred.

6. In **Rev. 4-5**, the twenty four elders are identified by the same things promised to the churches of Rev. 1-3: (a) seated on thrones (Rev. 4:4, cf. 3:21), (b) wearing white robes (Rev. 4:4, cf. 3: 5), (c) wearing gold crowns (Rev. 4:4, cf. 2:10, 3:11, 18), (d) which they cast before the throne of God, expressing their unworthiness and God's grace, Rev. 4:10-11, (e) kings and priests (thrones, crowns, 24 divisions of priests in the OT, 1 Chron. 24, cf. Rev. 1:6), and (f) elders, suggesting spiritual development, a title linked with the church. This suggests the twenty-four elders represent the church, who are seen in heaven in Rev. 4-19.

7. **1 Thess. 1:10** says we 'wait for His Son from heaven'. We are looking for the Son – not for signs, for Christ – not Antichrist.

8. **1 Thess. 1:10** says 'Jesus ... delivers us from the wrath to come'. The context is future – Jesus' return; the 'wrath to come' refers to the Day of the Lord (2 Thess. 5:1-10, 2 Thess. 2:2-12), the tribulation period.

9. **1 Thess. 5:9** says 'we are not appointed to wrath', the tribulation period of God's wrath (Rev. 6:17, 16:1, etc.).

10. **1 Thess. 2:19** describes Christ's coming as 'our hope and joy'. But if the church goes through the terrors of the tribulation, then the Lord's coming is a haunting nightmare, not a blessed hope.

11. **1 Thess. 4.13-17** is Paul's description of the rapture: 'we who are alive and remain shall be caught up'. Paul himself expected to be alive at the rapture (note the 'we' in 1 Cor. 15:52). Paul is not preparing for martyrdom in the tribulation; this suggests the rapture comes before it.

12. **1 Thess. 5:2** says the day of the Lord is coming as a thief in the night and like labour pains upon a pregnant woman. The Lord's coming is a surprise for believers (v1-2) and unbelievers (v3). This suggests a pre-tribulation rapture, because once the tribulation starts, believers will be able to count how many days it is before the Lord returns.

13. **The Restrainer** (2 Thess. 2:6-7) holding back Antichrist's arrival, taken out of the way, is best understood as the Holy Spirit in the church: powerful enough to stop Satan, opposing deception, both 'he' and 'it'[90].

14. **Luke 21:36** suggests an 'escape from all these things that will come to pass (i.e. the tribulation), and to stand before the Son of Man'.

15. In **John 14:2-3**, Christ promises, 'I will come again and receive you to Myself; that where I am, there you may be also', in 'My Father's house'. Christ is not talking of the believer's death, or the coming of the Holy Spirit, nor taking us to 'spiritual abodes within His own Person' (Gundry[91]). 'The simplest explanation is best: *my Father's house* refers to heaven' (Carson[92]). For Christ to come again, yet take us to heaven (not reign on earth) suggests a pre-tribulation rapture.

16. **Matt. 24:40-41** (two in the field, two at the mill, one taken, one left) describes a rapture, using the same word 'receive' as in John 14:2-3. As we saw in Ch. 79, this event is a surprise and occurs in conditions of peace and normality, i.e. pre-tribulation days. It is not a rapture of unbelievers (two raptures!), for all stand before Christ in Matt. 25:31ff.

17. **Imminency** (Christ could come at any time) is taught in Rom. 13:12, 1 Cor. 1:7, 16:22, Gal. 5:5, Phil. 3:20, 1 Thess. 1:10, 4:17, 1 Tim. 6:14, Tit. 2:13, Heb. 9:28, Rev. 22:20 (and see refs in Ch. 79).

18. **Interpretation**: a pre-tribulation rapture avoids fanciful allegorising and spiritualizing; it reads Scripture in a natural and normal way. Thus,

19. A pre-tribulation rapture maintains **a distinction between Israel and the church**; it holds to a national blessing of ethnic Israel.

20. **Purpose**: What is the purpose of a post-tribulation rapture, being instantly caught up, and then immediately returning? Nor is there any good biblical reason for the church to go through the tribulation.

ENDNOTES

[1] Bernard Ramm, *Protestant Christian Evidences*, Chicago: Moody Press, 1957, p232

[2] Peter W. Stoner, *Science Speaks*, Chicago: Moody Press, 1963, pp109-10

[3] William F. Albright, *Archaeology and the Religions of Israel*, Baltimore: The Johns Hopkins University Press, 1968, p176

[4] The title page of the KJV says that it was 'translated out of the Original Tongues, and with the former translations diligently compared and revised'. The KJV also originally included (in addition to the Apocrypha) over 8000 marginal notes giving alternative translations and the readings of different manuscripts. The translators wrote, 'doth not a margin do well to admonish the Reader to seek further, and not to conclude or dogmatize upon this or that peremptorily?'

[5] E. W. Rogers, "The Scriptures of Truth", *Treasury of Bible Doctrine*, Precious Seed Publications, 1977, p20

[6] F. F. Bruce, "The Scriptures", *The Faith – A Symposium of Bible Doctrine*, Kilmarnock: Ritchie, 1999, p18

[7] Augustine, *Letters*, 82.1.3

[8] Bruce Milne, *Know the Truth*, 3rd Ed., Nottingham: IVP, 2009, p23

[9] C. H. Mackintosh, "The Bible: Its Sufficiency and Supremacy", *The Mackintosh Treasury: Miscellaneous Writings*, Neptune, NJ: Loizeaux Brothers, 1976, p20

[10] F. F. Bruce, *The Books and the Parchments*, London: Marshall Pickering, 1991, p96

[11] B. M. Metzger, quoted in Lee Strobel, *The Case for Christ: a Journalist's Personal Investigation of the Evidence for Jesus*, Grand Rapids, MI: Zondervan, 1998, p67

[12] Fred Hoyle, *The Universe: Past and Present Reflections*, Annual Review of Astronomy and Astrophysics: 20:16 (1982)

[13] C. S. Lewis, *Mere Christianity*, New York: Harper Collins, 2001, p8

[14] G. R. Lewis, "God, Attributes of" in Walter A. Elwell, ed. *Evangelical Dictionary of Theology*, Grand Rapids, MI: Baker Book House, 1984, p451

[15] W. Hoste, *Studies in Bible Doctrine*, Bangalore: Scripture Literature Depot, 1932, p1

[16] T. C. Hammond, *In Understanding be Men*, London: IVP, 1954, p45

[17] C. S. Lewis, *A Grief Observed*, London: Faber & Faber, 2012, p33

[18] A. W. Tozer, *The Knowledge of the Holy*, Carlisle: OM, 1987, p78

[19] Graham Scroggie, *The Lord's Return*, London: Pickering and Inglis, n.d., p15

[20] Wayne Grudem, *Systematic Theology*, Leicester: IVP, 1994, p180

[21] Ibid, p178, 180

[22] Tozer, *The Knowledge of the Holy*, p17

[23] Millard Ericksen, *Christian Theology*, 2nd Ed., Grand Rapids, MI: Baker, 1998, p459

[24] C. S. Lewis, *The Screwtape Letters: Letters from a Senior to a Junior Devil*, London: HarperCollins UK, 2009, p8

[25] Quoted in Ravi Zacharias, *Can Man Live Without God?* Nashville: Thomas Nelson, 1994, pxviii

[26] Leon Morris, *The Lord from Heaven*, London: IVP, 1950, p51

[27] Hoste, *Studies in Bible Doctrine*, p67

[28] Steve Chalke and Alan Mann, *The Lost Message of Jesus*, 2003, Grand Rapids, MI: Zondervan, 2003, p182

[29] W. Wilcox, *Faith: a Symposium*, ed. F. A. Tatford, Kilmarnock: Ritchie, 1999, p90-91

[30] Wolfhart Pannenberg, *Prism Magazine*, March/April 1997

[31] Billy Graham, *The Holy Spirit*, London: William Collins, 1980, p100

[32] George J. Jennings, "An Ethnological Study of Glossolalia", *Journal of the American Scientific Affiliation*, March 1968

[33] Speaking in tongues is 'partially-developed speech', "Behavioral Science Research on the Nature of Glossolalia", *Journal of the American Scientific Affiliation*, September 1968; it is 'unintelligible babbling speech', William J. Samarin, "Variation and Variables in Religious Glossolalia", *Language in Society*, ed. Dell Haymes, Cambridge: Cambridge University Press, 1972, pp121-130.

[34] J. Mayhew & P. C. Salm, "Gender differences in anaerobic power tests", *European Journal of Applied Physiology*, 60(2), Feb. 1990, pp133-8

[35] Ø. Olsen, *Women and Men in Norway, What the Figures Say*, 2010, available as an e-book at the Norwegian Government website: https://www.regjeringen.no/globalassets/upload/bld/rapporter/2010/cedaw_rapporten/annex_3.pdf

[36] W. Wiersbe, *Be Rich (Ephesians)*, Colorado Spr.: David C. Cook, 2009, p107

[37] C. Thurman, *The Lies We Believe*, Nashville, TN: Nelson, 2003

[38] D. R. Davies, *On to Orthodoxy*, London: Hodder and Stoughton, 1940

[39] quoted in J. McDowell, *Christianity, A Ready Defence*, San Bernardino, CA: Here's Life, 1991, p454

[40] David Noebel, *The Battle for Truth*, Eugene, OR: Harvest House, 1982, p104

[41] Hammond, *In Understanding be Men*, p79

[42] Handley Moule, *Outlines of Christian Doctrine*, London: Hodder and Stoughton, 1890, p172

[43] R. Albert Mohler, "Preaching with the Culture in View," in *Preaching the Cross*, Wheaton, IL: Crossway, 2007, p81

[44] M. Bird, 'How God Became Jesus – and How I Came to Faith in Him', *Christianity Today*, April 16, 2014

[45] Hoste, *Studies*, pp172-3, 158

[46] Montague Goodman, "Sin", *The Faith – A Symposium*, p147

[47] Hoste, *Studies*, p107

[48] Hammond, *In Understanding be Men*, p148

[49] W. H. Griffith-Thomas, *The Principles of Theology*, London: Church Book Room, 1956, pxx

[50] Ludwig Ott, *Fundamentals of Catholic Dogma*, Ed. By James Canon Bastible, trans. by Patrick Lynch, St Louis: Herder, 1955, p264

[51] Dietrich Bonhoeffer, *The Cost of Discipleship*, New York: Touchstone, 1995, pp44-45

[52] C. S. Lewis, *Mere Christianity*, London: William Collins, 2002, pp47-48

[53] J. I. Packer, *Concise Theology*, Nottingham: IVP, 2011, pp28-29

[54] John Wesley, *A Plain Account of Christian Perfection* (1777)

[55] The Greek aorist tense is used in these verses, but the aorist is not a 'once-for-all', 'point' tense as has sometimes been taught. The Greek word 'aorist' means 'undefined' and while in the indicative it usually involves action in the past, its basic idea is an unspecified action, undefined in terms of whether it was 'once-for-all' or ongoing, starting or completed. For example, Romans 3:23 says 'all have sinned', but the aorist here does not mean we sinned 'once for all'.

[56] John Calvin, *Institutes of the Christian Religion*, Book 2, Chapter 7.12

[57] H. A. Ironside, *A Historical Sketch of the Brethren Movement*, Neptune, NJ: Loizeaux Brothers, 1985, pp211-212

[58] Max Lucado, *In the Grip of Grace*, Nashville: Nelson, 1998, p93

[59] Referring to taking Gk. *kai* as 'even': 'we should avoid the rare grammatical usages when the common ones make good sense' (S. Lewis Johnson, "Paul and the Israel of God", in *Essays in Honor of J. Dwight Pentecost*, eds. Stanley D. Toussaint and Charles H. Dyer, Chicago: Moody Press, 1986, p138).

[60] Kenneth Fleming, *Essentials of Missionary Service*, Carlisle: OM Publishing, 2000, p38

[61] Luther: 'the sole, uninterrupted, infallible mark of the church has always been the Word'

[62] Belgic Confession, Article 29: 'The Marks of the True Church'

[63] Edward M. Bounds, *Power Through Prayer*, Grand Rapids, MI: Baker, n.d., pp5, 7

[64] It is not clear whether 'breaking bread' in Acts 2:46 refers to the Lord's Supper or a normal meal.

[65] Paul Barnett, *1 Corinthians*, Fearn: Christian Focus, 2000, p263

[66] See *Do Not Quench the Spirit: a Biblical and Practical Guide to Participatory Church Gatherings*, North Lakes: Believers Publications, 2016

[67] Leon Morris, *1 Corinthians*, TNTC, Nottingham: IVP, 1985, p190

[68] Barnett, *1 Corinthians*, p263

[69] D. M. Lloyd-Jones, *Knowing the Times*, Edinburgh: Banner of Truth, 1989, pp195-6

70 I. H. Marshall, "1 Thessalonians", *New Bible Dictionary*, Leicester: IVP, 1994, p1284

71 Some argue that 1 Cor. 11:5 permits women to pray and prophecy in church, however the context here is not the church (note the contrast with verses 17ff). As B. B. Warfield writes, 'there is nothing said about the church in the passage or in the context. The word "church" does not occur until the 16th verse ... There is no reason whatever for believing that 'praying and prophesying' in the church is meant. Neither was an exercise confined to the church' ("Paul on Women Speaking in Church", *The Presbyterian*, October 30, 1919). The same point is made by J. N. Darby (*Synopsis of the Books of the Bible*, Vol. 4, Stow Hill Bible and Tract Depot, 1958, p175), W. E. Vine (*First Corinthians*, Oliphants, 1951, p147), W. MacDonald (*Believers Bible Commentary*, Nelson, 1995, p 1785), and R. C. H. Lenski (*1 and 2 Corinthians*, 1963, Augsburg, pp 436-7).

72 James Denney, "The Epistles to the Thessalonians", *The Expositor's Bible*, London: Hodder and Stoughton, 1902, p244

73 Augustine, *The City of God*, Book 20, chapter 30

74 J. C. Ryle, "Scattered Israel to be Gathered", in *Coming Events and Present Duties: being Plain Papers on Prophecy*, Memphis, TN: Bottom of the Hill, 2012

75 From a homily preached by Pope Francis in St. Martha's House, Rome, on 19th September, 2014.

76 See *The Most Amazing Prophecy in the Bible: Daniel's Prophecy of the Seventy Sevens*, North Lakes: Believers Publications, 2015

77 A. C. Gaebelein, *A Key to the Visions and Prophecies of the Book of Daniel*, New York: Publication Office, "Our Hope", 1911, pp129-130

78 Alva J. McClain, *Daniel's Prophecy of the Seventy Weeks*, BMH Books, 2007, p10

79 The 'abomination of desolation' was not set up in AD67-70. Some claim the Roman ensigns, but Christ did not call such Roman emblems 'abominations' in Matt. 22:20-21, nor did He return *immediately* after AD70 (Matt. 24:29).

80 Luther, *The Jews and their Lies*, 1543

81 Grant R. Osborne, *Romans*, Downer's Grove, IL: IVP, 2010, p306

82 Anthony Hoekema, an amillennialist, writes, 'Amillennialists believe that the return of Christ will be preceded by certain signs: for example, the preaching of

the gospel to all the nations, the conversion of the fullness of Israel, the great apostasy, the great tribulation and the coming of the Antichrist' (*The Meaning of the Millennium*, 1977). See also Berkhof (*Systematic Theology*, p700). Charles Hodge, a postmillennialist writes, 'those days of tribulation which the Bible seems to teach are to immediately precede the coming of the Lord', (*Systematic Theology*, 1871-3, reprinted Eerdmans: Grand Rapids, MI, 1977, 3:812). For Charles Ryrie (a premillennialist) see *Basic Theology*, Victor Books, 1986, p464.

[83] John F. Walvoord, *The Rapture Question*, Grand Rapids: Zondervan, 1979, p158

[84] The aorist tense in Rev. 6:17 ('the wrath *has come*') does not mean 'is about to come'. Rather, as Alford writes, 'the virtually perfect sense of the aor. *elthen* here can hardly be questioned' (*The Greek New Testament*, London: Rivingtons, 1875, Vol. 4, p622). One quarter of humanity dies (Rev. 6:8); this is the wrath of God.

[85] Other OT references that show that Matt. 24:31 refers to a Jewish re-gathering include Deut 4:32, Isa. 13:5 ('the end of the heavens'), Isa. 27:12-13 ('the great trumpet' that re-gathers Israel), and Isa. 11:11-12, Jer. 49:32 ('the four winds') and see also Zech 2:10 (LXX, translating Zech. 2:6, which reads, 'Up, up, flee from the land of the north, says the Lord, for I will gather you from the four winds of the heavens, says the Lord).

[86] *Thesaurus Linguae Graecae* (TLG) produces 91 pages of citations of various forms of the word *apantesis* from several centuries before and after Paul, and only a minority of references describe formal receptions. See Michael R. Crosby, "Hellenistic Formal Receptions and Paul's use of APANTHSIS in 1 Thessalonians 4:17", *Bulletin for Biblical Research* 4 (1994), p19

[87] Wayne Grudem, *Systematic Theology*, Leicester: IVP, 1994, p1100ff.

[88] Berkhof, *Systematic Theology*, Grand Rapids, MI: Eerdmans, 1939, p696

[89] D. A. Carson, "Matthew", *Expositors Bible Commentary*, Vol. 8, Grand Rapids, MI: Zondervan, 1984, p490

[90] The Holy Spirit is referred to elsewhere as both 'it' (*pneuma*, Spirit, is neuter in Greek) but also referred to in the masculine as well (John 14:26, 15:26, etc.)

[91] Robert Gundry, *The Church and the Tribulation*, Grand Rapids: Zondervan, 1973, p154

[92] D. A. Carson, *The Gospel according to John*, PNTC, Grand Rapids, MI: Eerdmans, 1990, p489

OTHER BOOKS BY THE SAME AUTHOR

Matthew's Messiah: a Guide to Matthew's Gospel

The Most Amazing Prophecy in the Bible: Daniel's Prophecy of the Seventy Sevens

Is the Bible Really the Word of God? The Doctrine of Scripture

Do Not Quench the Spirit: a Biblical and Practical Guide to Participatory Church Gatherings

www.ingramcontent.com/pod-product-compliance
Lightning Source LLC
Chambersburg PA
CBHW070425010526
44118CB00014B/1911